Managing Yourself
In A Week

Martin Manser

Martin Manser is an expert communicator with a unique combination of skills and experience. He has compiled or edited over 200 reference books on the English language, Bible reference and business skills in a 35-year professional career. He is an English-language specialist and teaches English to business colleagues. Participants in his courses find them to be a safe place to ask questions and for their confidence to grow. Since 2002, he has also been a Language Consultant and Trainer, leading training courses in business communications for national and international companies and organizations on communications, project management and time management.

www.martinmanser.co.uk

Managing Yourself

Martin Manser

Teach Yourself®

IN A WEEK

First published in Great Britain in 2016 by Hodder and Stoughton. An Hachette UK company.

First published in US in 2016.

Copyright © Martin Manser 2016

The right of Martin Manser to be identified as the Author of the Work has been asserted by him in accordance with the Copyright, Designs and Patents Act 1988.

Database right Hodder & Stoughton (makers)

British Library Cataloguing in Publication Data: a catalogue record for this title is available from the British Library.

Library of Congress Catalog Card Number: on file.

9781473607569

eISBN: 9781473607576

1

The publisher has used its best endeavours to ensure that any website addresses referred to in this book are correct and active at the time of going to press. However, the publisher and the author have no responsibility for the websites and can make no guarantee that a site will remain live or that the content will remain relevant, decent or appropriate.

The publisher has made every effort to mark as such all words which it believes to be trademarks. The publisher should also like to make it clear that the presence of a word in the book, whether marked or unmarked, in no way affects its legal status as a trademark.

Every reasonable effort has been made by the publisher to trace the copyright holders of material in this book. Any errors or omissions should be notified in writing to the publisher, who will endeavour to rectify the situation for any reprints and future editions.

Typeset by Cenveo® Publisher Services.

Printed and bound in Great Britain by CPI Group (UK) Ltd., Croydon, CR0 4YY.

John Murray Learning policy is to use papers that are natural, renewable and recyclable products and made from wood grown in sustainable forests. The logging and manufacturing processes are expected to conform to the environmental regulations of the country of origin.

Hodder & Stoughton Ltd
Carmelite House
50 Victoria Embankment
London EC4Y 0DZ
www.hodder.co.uk

Also available in ebook

Contents

Introduction

Congratulations! You've been promoted to manager. However, after all the excitement has lessened, you begin to question yourself: ...can you achieve ... are you really equipped? This book considers one important aspect of being a manager: being able to manage yourself. For example, you may be poor at clarifying priorities or have weak time-management skills.

The first step in managing yourself effectively is to become aware of yourself and evaluate your strengths and weaknesses. Maintaining focus on the tasks in hand is vital, alongside allowing opportunities for you to 'catch up' and process what is going on in your life. Asking what the next step is moves you on from inertia.

Good time management is an essential skill in being an effective manager, and a chapter is devoted to becoming more organized. This explains better planning and setting priorities, shows how to deal with time wasters, and gives practical steps on maintaining a diary and to-do lists. Further chapters consider techniques such as managing your mind, discussing thinking positively in developing strategies and making good decisions, managing emotions, not by ignoring them but allowing them to be expressed appropriately, and explaining how to increase confidence, deal with nerves and motivate yourself.

The final chapters consider developing trust and respect. This can be done through building strong relationships by applying good listening skills, as seen in working with your boss and colleagues. They also consider the importance of having good relationships outside work. The final chapter, on managing stress, invites you to look at what produces stress in you and discusses ways of dealing with its consequences. **Managing Yourself in a Week** offers handy guidelines that will enable you to take a grip on yourself and re-evaluate your way of working and your priorities in life. It is a quick and reliable guide to the basics of self-management in the world of work.

Each day of the week covers a different area and follows the same structure. The day begins with an introduction to that day's topic. Then the main material explains the key lessons by clarifying important principles. These are backed up by tips and case studies. Each day concludes with a summary, an exercise and multiple-choice questions to reinforce the learning points.

The principles I outline here are the fruit of over 35 years in business, particularly in the area of communications, and over 12 years in leading courses on business communications. As I have reflected on participants' responses to the training courses I have led, two comments keep recurring: 'You gave me more confidence' and 'Today was a refresher course'. My hope, therefore, is that as you read and act on what I write, this will be a refresher course that will give you fresh confidence to manage yourself effectively.

Martin Manser

SUNDAY

Know yourself well

Today we will consider what you are like as a person. We will look at:

- Your goals and values
- Your skills and abilities
- Your achievements, successes and failures
- Your preferred style of working

We will consider these with a view to thinking which areas are your strengths and which areas you may need to develop further.

We will also consider:

- The difference between managing and leading
- The difference between being efficient and being effective

My aim is to help you to:

- Understand the issues facing you and prepare the ground
- Develop your skills, techniques and knowledge
- Motivate yourself

Let's begin with a story ...

Another day had gone badly. Michael had had two rushed meetings that he was supposed to have led, but hadn't really had time to gather his thoughts for, and an appraisal that he hadn't prepared for at all. Finally, he'd been asked to come up with some strategic, long-term thinking. He hadn't even begun to tackle the main task that he had been assigned to that day (although at least he had tried to do some planning for it!).

Mike had been promoted to manager of a new department, and he knew he wasn't coping. He seemed to spend all his time – and energy – lurching from one crisis to another. His nerves were constantly on edge, his stress levels were high, and his self-confidence (such as it was) seemed to be draining away by the day. He had started off with high hopes of changing things – changing lots of things: structures, priorities... Maybe he had begun too strongly and hadn't spent time building good relationships with his colleagues, somehow expecting that they would agree with all his plans immediately. And now everything seemed to be failing. Even at home, his relationships were strained and uneasy. He was spending too much time at the office, so he hardly saw his children during the week. Even on weekends, something urgent often seemed to come up unexpectedly. As for his relationship with his wife, well...

Deep within himself, when he had a few moments to stop and think, Mike knew something was wrong. He couldn't keep on blaming the people around him. He knew he had to sort himself out.

Do you identify with Mike? Maybe he hadn't had enough training for his present position; maybe he'd been promoted to the level of his incompetence.[1] Certainly he hadn't learnt to

---

[1] The so-called Peter Principle: 'In a hierarchy, every employee tends to rise to the level of his incompetence.' This semi-scientific statement was formulated by the Canadian educator Dr Laurence J Peter (1919–90) who with Raymond Hull (1919–85) wrote the book *The Peter Principle – Why Things Always Go Wrong*, published in 1969. The Principle holds that so long as the managers are competent, they will continue to be promoted. Eventually they will reach a position which is beyond them and they will not progress any further.

manage his time, nor how to delegate tasks to others. In brief, he hadn't learnt to manage himself.

Being able to manage yourself begins with being aware of yourself, what kind of person you are.

Self-awareness

Your goals

Today I want to encourage you to think more deeply about your life and the kind of person you are.

The US leadership expert, John Maxwell (in *The 21 Indispensable Qualities of a Leader*; Thomas Nelson, 1999), asks three questions to help you work out a personal vision for your life:

● What makes you cry?
● What makes you dream?
● What gives you energy?

It can be useful to spend some time responding to these questions. Then ask yourself whether the main part of your life actually matches your answers. If it doesn't, then think what you could do to change your life.

You might be in a job in which you feel fulfilled: that is good! Or you might be in a job that you cannot change and is in conflict with, for example, a deep desire you have to help needy people. Because you cannot discern a way out of that job in the foreseeable future (and you've responsibilities with family, bills to pay...), you might consider volunteering with a local charity one evening a week or at weekends to channel that desire to help others.

Your values

What motivates you? What drives you? What underlying values and beliefs do you hold?

● Do you have integrity?
● Are you honest and firm in having strong moral principles that you follow? Or are you pretending to be someone you're not?

- Do you work too hastily to try to save time or money but, in doing so, are you less thorough than you know you should be?
- Do you guard what enters your mind and take control of your thoughts?

Other aspects you need to consider are:

- Do you enjoy your position of power and authority as a manager?
- Do you have many grand ideas, but do they remain only as ideas that do not become real?
- How important is money to you?
- Are you ambitious?
- How important are your family relationships to you?
- Are you trustworthy? You will only inspire trust in others if you yourself are reliable and responsible. If you say you will do something by a certain time, do you do so? (Colleagues will notice if you are constantly late in meeting deadlines, and so will take that as permission that they can act similarly.)
- Are you straightforward and avoid acting unfairly or dishonestly?
- Do you start projects with good ideas and enthusiasm, but fail to follow them through? Or do you continue with projects until they are successfully completed?
- Do you want to learn and grow as a person, or have you reached a plateau?
- What is your prevailing attitude in life and work?
  - Positive? Confident? Committed? Enthusiastic? Affirming? Caring?
  - Unmotivated? Disengaged? Negative? Cynical? Unappreciated? Frustrated? Pessimistic? Rude?

Your skills and abilities

As a manager, you need various core qualities of skills and behaviour. Mark yourself on a scale of 1 to 5 of how you think you perform on the following (1 = poor, 5 = excellent). Then ask a trusted colleague to mark you, and check to see if your scores agree.

		You	Colleague

1 Good with people: approachable and able to get on with others, to motivate others and respect colleagues ❏ ❏

2 Good team leader: respecting others, recognizing colleagues' skills and focusing on their strengths ❏ ❏

3 Good negotiation skills: able to secure win–win situations ❏ ❏

4 Good skills of delegation to trusted colleagues: empowering them, to avoid becoming stressed by taking too much on yourself ❏ ❏

5 Good at resolving conflict ❏ ❏

6 Good listener: showing empathy towards others ❏ ❏

7 Good computer skills, e.g. on spreadsheets ❏ ❏

8 Good manager of your time: good at planning ❏ ❏

9 Committed to your work: having an active, positive belief in it; believing in your company, products/services and staff (on the basis that enthusiasm is contagious) ❏ ❏

10 Good general management skills: able to think strategically, chair meetings well, take the initiative and make decisions ❏ ❏

11 Organized: someone who is careless or sloppy in their professional life will not be a good manager ❏ ❏

12 Good numeracy skills: being proficient with figures; able to manage budgets ❏ ❏

13 Good business sense: take advantage of opportunities, keep an eye on costs ❏ ❏

14 Having an eye for detail: someone who is thorough and meticulous is needed (however, also see the next quality) ❏ ❏

15 Able to see the big picture: someone who only sees details will quickly become overwhelmed and unable to see things in perspective and move forward ❏ ❏

16 Able to keep track of different processes ('keep several balls in the air') at the same time, able to document progress clearly ❏ ❏

SUNDAY

MONDAY

TUESDAY

WEDNESDAY

THURSDAY

FRIDAY

SATURDAY

17 Proactive: staying in control and thinking
ahead ☐ ☐
18 Able to analyse matters and discern what is
significant ☐ ☐
19 Creative and flexible in finding solutions to
difficulties: what worked three years ago might
not work now ☐ ☐
20 Able to stay focused on the goal: patient and
determined ☐ ☐
21 Able to focus on the needs of your clients/
customers ☐ ☐
22 Able to recruit and maintain (and retain!)
good staff: develop, train or coach other
colleagues well ☐ ☐
23 Results-orientated ☐ ☐
24 Considerate of the environment, workplace and
staff well-being ☐ ☐

(We will consider many of these in more detail throughout this week.)

Looking at these results:

● Consider which skills are most important in your role at the present time
● What are your three greatest strengths (the ones you got the highest scores for)? You should concentrate on ('play to') your strengths as far as you can
● Which are your three greatest weaknesses (the ones you got the lowest scores for)? Consider these points carefully:
  – Some of your weaknesses are a necessary part of your job and you need to recognize them as areas to develop and work at
  – Others may not be an integral part of your job, so try to match your weaknesses with the strengths of colleagues

For example, I am good with words: writing books has been my livelihood for three decades, which I have always done on the computer in Word. But I also have to be reasonably good with numbers to ensure that the books I write are not too short or too long, and also that they are profitable as far as I can control.

I also lead training courses as part of my work. So while the skills in Word come relatively easily, I have had to teach myself skills in Excel and PowerPoint to reach a more than basic level in those. However, areas that are not central to my job – for example, designing book covers for digital versions of my books – I delegate to a colleague who is much more skilled than me.

Your achievements in life

- What have you achieved in your life so far? Think of things related to work and also those not related to work. Ask friends and colleagues. Also, look back at the past few years and consider where you have been successful
- What weaknesses are you aware of in your life? They may be to do with certain business skills, e.g. that you only see the detail and do not see the wider situation as a whole. Or if the weaknesses are more personal, it can be helpful to share those with a trusted colleague or friend
- People often say you need to learn from your failures, and that is true. But you also need to learn from your successes. Why were these achievements successful? Can you repeat some of the elements that led to that success?
- Accept responsibility for your life. You cannot always blame your circumstances on other people. Sometimes we are the ones at fault and we need to be humble enough to admit our mistakes, focus on the future, and move on to the next step

Your style of living ... and working

Think through the following:

- Which energizes you more: being with other people or being by yourself?
- When responding to new ideas, do you react spontaneously ('thinking on your feet') or do you prefer to take your time to reply?
- Do you work best in normal, regular and highly structured patterns of work or does an immediate deadline or crisis bring out the best in you?

- Do you have interests outside work that are important to you?
- Do you work best as a leader or as a second-in-command?
- Do you work best alone or as a member of a team?
- Do you work best in a large company/organization or in a small one?
- How open are you about sharing your life with other people?

A change of lifestyle

Jack enjoyed his work, but gradually it took over his whole life. Eventually he became ill. He consulted a doctor, who advised a complete change of lifestyle. He needed to leave work punctually, eat a healthier diet and have more sleep. He also realized he needed to spend much more time with his family (and switch his mobile off over mealtimes and when reading his young children their bedtime story) and pursue ordinary leisure activities. So he took up badminton and played one evening a week. Over time, Jack's life improved considerably: he achieved more and became a much more rounded person.

Sharing yourself

When you are new to a job, how much do you share of yourself to your colleagues? What you are good at, what you are not so good at, personal matters such as your birthday?

As you get to know colleagues more, you gradually disclose more of yourself.[2]

Accept yourself

For years, I was introverted, and no number of people telling me to become less so helped at all. Gradually, over the years, I relaxed and found my own identity. Accept yourself.

2 The framework of the 'Johari window' is helpful here. It is based on a window divided into four panes representing the four types of personal awareness: open, hidden, blind and unknown. The Johari window is named after *Jo*seph Luft and *Har*ry Ingham, the American psychologists who developed it in 1955. It is widely used to promote improved understanding in corporate environments and in self-help groups.

We have all had difficult experiences in life up to this point; the key thing is to how we respond to them. Some may have been particularly difficult and we may need to seek professional help to deal with them. People who are brave enough to pluck up the courage to seek help often find that it helps them enormously, and enables them to go on to do things they previously found difficult or even impossible. Stop thinking so much about how other people perceive you. Don't let their opinions stifle your own personality, style and view of the world. Be yourself – and be kind to yourself too.

Managing and leading

What are the differences between managing and leading? Here is a rough definition: *managing is turning leadership into action*. Let me explain that in more detail: leaders set a particular course: we're going to expand into the Latin American market. Managers put that into action: we're going to understand the culture, build a base, recruit staff there and implement a whole range of other activities to make the basic idea of 'expanding into the Latin American market' a reality.

So leaders set the overall direction, guide, influence, and give vision; managers implement that vision, working out the detail in terms of organizing people, planning and budgeting. You will probably have agreed with this last sentence. However, are you aware that there is another aspect of leadership: that of emotions? Leaders appeal to the emotions to set a course of change, wanting to inspire people to follow a vision. Managers, in contrast it seems, have the less exciting task of ensuring that the work, in all its detail, is completed.

In practice, however, the distinction between 'leader' and 'manager' may not be so clear cut. Your role may be 'team leader', and your duties will concentrate on the detailed tasks, systems and processes needed to ensure the work is completed. However, you will also need leadership skills to motivate your team to achieve these goals.

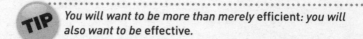

TIP *You will want to be more than merely* efficient: *you will also want to be* effective.

Working efficiently and effectively

Note there is a difference between working efficiently and effectively: *efficient* means 'well organized, achieving results with minimal waste of resources such as time and money. *Effective* is more than that: it means also achieving the right results. You can do the wrong thing efficiently, but as managers you want to be *effective*.

For example, I was discussing auditing procedures with a colleague in the banking industry. She said they were *efficient* – it was relatively easy to define tasks that satisfied all the requirements ('ticked all the boxes'). When I asked if such tasks would be *effective* in moving the bank forward, however, she was uncertain.

Remember: As a manager, you will want to be more than merely *efficient*: you will also want to be *effective*.

Measuring your success

It is important to note specific actions throughout this week. Where possible, action points should be SMART:

S   **S**pecific: defining the desired results
M   **M**easurable: quantifiable so that you know whether the objectives have been reached
A   **A**chievable: realistic objectives that are not too easy, but will develop and challenge ('stretch') your resources and skills
R   **R**elevant: are concerned with your life and work
T   **T**imed: giving a date for completion

Some commentators add:
E   **E**valuated: progress on achieving SMART actions is reviewed at a future meeting
R   **R**eported: evaluated progress is reported and recorded

Summary

Today we have begun to lay the foundation for managing yourself more effectively by looking at your life. Important factors include:

- self awareness
- efficient and effective working

Exercise

Answer the following questions, taking into account what we have considered today.

1 Are you content where you currently are as a person or have you reached a plateau and would like to learn more to grow?

2 Do you have a clear sense of purpose in life and at work?

3 What are your strengths? Choose one and consider how you can develop it to become even more proficient.

4 Which one quality do you need to cultivate more? What are the next steps you need to take to do this? Make sure your action points are SMART.

5 What interests outside work could you develop more?

SUNDAY

MONDAY

TUESDAY

WEDNESDAY

THURSDAY

FRIDAY

SATURDAY

Fact-check

1. In order to manage yourself better, you need to:
   a) ignore your life ❏
   b) consider your life ❏
   c) remain the same ❏
   d) check social media websites constantly ❏

2. Considering your goals and values is:
   a) useful if you have the time ❏
   b) a waste of time ❏
   c) an important first step to managing yourself ❏
   d) helpful just to discuss with others ❏

3. 'I am prepared to change my life in order to manage myself better':
   a) true ❏
   b) false ❏
   c) I'm not sure ❏
   d) I don't care ❏

4. To reflect on your attitude at work is:
   a) too serious ❏
   b) useful if you have the time ❏
   c) a waste of time ❏
   d) important ❏

5. When you consider areas that are your strengths, you should:
   a) deny you ever have them ❏
   b) delegate them to others to increase their competence ❏
   c) identify and then forget them ❏
   d) make sure you use them in your job ❏

6. When you consider areas that are your weaknesses, you should:
   a) have training in each area to increase your competences significantly ❏
   b) ignore them and deal only with your strengths ❏
   c) distinguish between areas that are important in your job and areas that you can delegate to others ❏
   d) delegate each one to someone else ❏

7. You should learn from your successes as well as your failures:
   a) false ❏
   b) true ❏
   c) 'I have had no failures' ❏
   d) 'I have had no successes' ❏

8. In your work, you want to:
   a) be efficient ❏
   b) be effective ❏
   c) be efficient and effective ❏
   d) go home early every day ❏

9. S and T in SMART actions stand for:
   a) sensible and timed ❏
   b) strategic and technological ❏
   c) specific and trusted ❏
   d) specific and timed ❏

10. Now that you have completed this chapter, you are going to:
    a) choose one area of your life to work on ❏
    b) try to find ten things you can change this week ❏
    c) do nothing ❏
    d) read it again ten more times ❏

SUNDAY

MONDAY

TUESDAY

WEDNESDAY

THURSDAY

FRIDAY

SATURDAY

MONDAY

Manage your focus clearly

Introduction

Today, we move on from knowing yourself to beginning to tackle how you can make progress and develop as an effective manager.

We will look at:

- staying focused in your work, working when you can concentrate best and undertaking your main task(s) with few distractions
- making time to think creatively about future goals, evaluating your present position and then beginning to make changes happen
- giving your mind some 'breathing space', allowing you to digest all that is happening to you and coming up with fresh thoughts and ideas
- growing personally

SUNDAY

MONDAY

TUESDAY

WEDNESDAY

THURSDAY

FRIDAY

SATURDAY

Stay focused

Today, my main task is to write a third of this chapter: I know from past experience that it takes about three good mornings' work to write each chapter in this book.

However, there are so many other things I could do: I have already taken my wife to work, and a car surprised me by its speed on a roundabout, so I could dwell on that. I also have many other items on my to-do list: check my accounts online; prepare for a meeting tomorrow (I started my preparation for that yesterday, but other thoughts have occurred to me since then); send out a marketing email; expect a colleague to phone to discuss future collaboration; check some material on a reference book; and respond to or initiate several other minor emails for personal arrangements for a family party.

I am now faced with a basic choice:

1 I could first deal with all the relatively minor things that need to be done (ideally most of them today) and then pursue my main task – writing this text – or:
2 I could pursue writing my main text first of all, and then try to fit in as many of the other things as possible, as time permits during the rest of the day.

I have chosen 2: my intention is to work on this chapter for a good two hours and then take a break. During my break, I will order most of my other remaining tasks, including any others that have since come in from my emails, and tackle them in order.

The criteria I work by are as follows:

1 Know when – which time of day and which day of the week – you work best.
2 I know that I work best first thing in the morning and also early in the week (for me, Monday and Tuesday). I therefore protect that time as far as possible in order to complete my main task(s). So my Monday and Tuesday mornings are special times that I guard as I am very unwilling to see them wasted.

Pursue the main task first.

The main task may be the one that will take the longest, or it could also be the most difficult, the most important or the one that I least want to tackle. I consider this last aspect especially important. Each day brings work that I don't particularly want to do, so I make myself undertake that as soon as I can. In this way, I feel psychologically better as I have a sense of achievement after I have completed it, or at least dealt with its most difficult or most significant part. (I know that – for me – the longer I postpone tackling tasks I don't want to do, the more difficult they seem.)

I was once teaching this principle to a colleague who gave talks at weekends, so Monday is her rest day and Tuesday the first day of her working week. Knowing that she worked best in the mornings, I asked how she had spent the previous Tuesday morning, expecting her to say she prepared her talks then. However, she replied that that was when she went for travel inoculations for her next foreign trip. I suggested that that was not the best use of her Tuesday mornings and that should be done on, for example, a Thursday afternoon. I spoke to her three months later and she was now using Tuesday to prepare her talks.

Pursue the other, less important, tasks later.

In other words, keep the main thing the 'main thing'. The main thing for me today is to complete about one third of this chapter in order to maintain the schedule that I have set myself, which is in keeping with the publisher's deadline and the deadlines I have set myself for my other work.

If I had pursued my tasks the other way and undertaken the less important items first, I know what would have happened. (I have done this extremely occasionally, just to see the results ... I and don't recommend it at all.) If I had pursued all the other relatively minor tasks first:

I would have become side-tracked from my main task of writing this chapter. I would then have had had only a small amount of time left at the end of the day, so I would not have actually completed my main work.

I would have become further side-tracked. I would answer an email and then another email could come in, and I would say to myself, 'While I am answering this one, I might as well just do that one too.'

I would not have built up any momentum in my work. It is true that I would have ticked off many (relatively minor) tasks, but because each one is comparatively short, I would never have picked up the pace and speed I need to get through a significant amount of work as easily as I would have done if I had started my major task first.

So, the guideline here is: concentrate on – pursue – your main task vigorously. Don't get side-tracked or distracted from your main task. Of course, this is only a guideline: there will be times when a crisis occurs and plans have to be abandoned or modified. It is also worth scheduling time to work on your minor tasks at a later date so that you can be certain they get done and don't become crises themselves.

Note that while completing your major task, switch off your mobile phone and emails. You don't want to be distracted.

See also Chapter Three (Tuesday) on priorities.

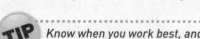

TIP *Know when you work best, and use that time for the task that is the most difficult or the one you least want to do.*

Make time to think

I am convinced that we spend too little time thinking. We are so busy with the present that we don't spend enough time thinking whether we are spending our time productively. To put it in terms of Chapter One (Sunday), we may just about be efficient but we don't take time to see whether we are being effective. Indeed, one of the Seven 7s at the end of this book is that you schedule three substantial thinking sessions into your diary (three on the basis that two might get swept away by the urgent).

So what are you to think about? Here are some guidelines:

● Set long-term goals. What are your company's or organization's long-term aims? If you don't have any then you are sure to fulfil them, because they are non-existent! If you do have such goals, are your present policies likely to achieve them?

● Dream dreams. It's amazing how random thoughts or wishes can turn into big things. If you want to do something, do it. I did this once with dictionaries. I remember it now. Our daughter was still a baby. I was thinking about words beginning with the letter 'G' ... a few were interesting, *galore* ('plenty') is an example of an adjective that follows the noun it refers to (*whisky galore!*); *galvanize* ('stir into action') is an example of a word named after a person, Luigi *Galvani*. I suddenly had a brainwave – what if on every page of a dictionary we could highlight a few words that were remarkable in a distinctive way? And so the idea came about for a book that I later worked on with my friend and colleague Nigel Turton. It was originally published by Penguin as the *Wordmaster Dictionary* and sold well. It is an 'ordinary' dictionary, but on nearly every page alongside main dictionary entries we highlighted in a boxed panel a particular word with an interesting history, idiom, grammatical feature, point of usage, etc. My creativity paid off!

'What is the hardest task in the world? To think'

Ralph Waldo Emerson, 1803–82, US poet, essayist and philosopher

● Undertake a SWOT analysis: This is a technique to help you develop creative thinking in a business context. In it, you analyse where your business/project/department is going, and it helps you make sure you've got a strong strategy

Strengths	What are you better at than your competitors? What is your USP (unique selling proposition)?
Weaknesses	What do your competitors perceive as your weaknesses? Is morale low? Is your leadership committed? Are there gaps in the skills of your colleagues?
Opportunities	What changes in the market or changes in lifestyle can you exploit to maximize your profits?
Threats	Is the market for your product declining? Are key colleagues on the verge of leaving? Is your financial backing stable?

Conducting a SWOT analysis to analyse where your company/organization currently stands will help you think creatively. This may lead to your adopting a new strategy that your competitors have not thought of. For example, in 2004 Amazon set up a covert team to unsettle its own business; the outcome of that team's work was the Kindle.

Other things you may need to be aware of:

● Realize that your role as manager is more than just making sure things run smoothly. You also need to initiate change. This may mean challenging the current way of doing things
● Evaluate what you are doing; question it. You are not being awkward for the sake of it, you are checking to see if you could work more effectively. Allow creative ideas, which may then generate other more realistic options
● Always conclude your thinking time by asking, 'What are the next steps? What practical thing do I/we need to do to begin to put our plans into action?' You might need to discuss your ideas with senior managers, or write an email to a colleague with your thoughts. In other words, do something. Focus on the next thing you need to do in order to achieve your goal, to make your goal a reality

My son Ben wanted to go to Japan so he realized he needed to learn Japanese. He therefore arranged lessons with a friend of my wife's every Thursday evening for two years. His desire to go to Japan would have remained a dream if he hadn't taken the initiative and done something about it

Give your mind some 'breathing space'

As well as blocking out time to think, give yourself time to unwind and relax – time to recover from the stresses of work. Plan in 'down' time, time when you are not concentrating. Commuting by train can provide an opportunity to do this. For example, yesterday I had meetings in London. On my hour-long journey into London by train, I was engaged in background reading for this book. However, on my return trip, I deliberately decided not to read anything. I chatted to the man sitting next to me for a while and, after he got off the train at a station earlier than mine, I had some ideas, which I wrote down, following up on ways to tackle the project we had discussed at my earlier business meeting.

Your subconscious needs time to process all that is going on. We are inundated with so much – too much – information that we don't take time to digest properly what we are taking in. I think it is often more a matter of the *quality* of information, not the *quantity*. There is sometimes no shortage of information (although, on occasions, I realize that we are missing vital pieces of information), but what we lack is the breathing space for our minds, to allow our brain the freedom to think creatively. We need to give ourselves the opportunity to reflect, allowing our subconscious to explore fresh possibilities and solve problems.

I expect you are familiar with this: you wake up in the morning and think of the answer to a problem that you had failed to solve the previous day, despite giving it a lot of thought then. Or you go for a walk, or are on holiday, and suddenly and unexpectedly you think of an original idea or a fresh insight that is just what you need.

You can get a lot achieved if you give your brain time to think.

Are you growing as a person?

Confession time: about fifteen years ago, I felt I had stopped growing inwardly as a person. It wasn't that I thought I knew it all, I knew I didn't. But I had lost that fresh motivation in my work. It was then that I noticed friends and colleagues around me were saying things like, 'When you retire, what will happen to all the knowledge you have built up?' and, 'Martin, I've learnt a lot from you.' I then began to realize that maybe I had accumulated certain competences and knowledge, so I started to think in different directions: that as well as writing, maybe I could pursue training and teaching in some of the skills I had learnt.

That experience also taught me the need to reflect regularly (for example, at least once a month) on the nature of my work and whether what I was doing was stretching me. Ideally, discuss with colleagues the trends in your industry. Pursue training, read books like this one, consult websites listed in the Seven 7s resources at the end of this book; discuss with colleagues the trends in your industry; question assumptions in an effort to find fresh approaches.

If you have had a failure or a great disappointment, then try to return quickly to your normal activities or your previous level of enthusiasm. Don't let one negative experience affect the whole of your life. In golf, if you have a bad score at one hole, you still need to keep playing the rest of the game. Bring that theory into your day-to-day life. The ability to recover from difficulties in life wins admiration from others: people greatly respect those who have learnt to come back from an unpleasant experience.

Discuss things with a coach or mentor

Discuss all these matters with your coach or mentor, if you have one. If you don't, encourage your company or organization to set up coaching or mentoring or, if that is not possible, find someone you can discuss your thoughts with. Listen to their comments and observations. (We will discuss listening in greater depth on **Friday**.) Be open to constructive criticism to help you grow as a person. All the time, do what you can to work well and grow as a person. Life will never be perfect. Work from where you are now. And remember, you may need to adjust your expectations.

Discussions with a mentor

Sarah met regularly with Janet, her mentor. Janet wasn't Sarah's line manager, so Sarah felt able to discuss her work freely and confidentially with Janet. In particular, Sarah was able to talk through not only her short- and mid-term training needs, but also her long-term career aspirations.

Janet was a good listener: she noted what Sarah was saying, and also what she was not saying. She could 'read (and listen) between the lines' and ask good questions. Janet could discern things that Sarah was not aware of.

Janet brought an objective perspective and helped Sarah see herself as a whole person, as well as offering guidance on the development of her future career.

Summary

Today we have emphasized the need to:

- Think when – what time of day and which day(s) of the week – you work best
- Focus your mind on one particular task
- Complete that task as far as possible, and only then undertake other less important tasks
- Think: give yourself the opportunity to think creatively about your life
- Act: at the end of any significant time of thinking, ask yourself, 'What is the next step I must undertake to advance this thought to turn it into reality?'

Exercise

1 Look at your to-do list. Think which task is the longest/most important/the most difficult/the one you least want to tackle.

2 Write down when – what time of day and which day(s) of the week – you work best.

3 Revise your diary such that you deliberately try to deal with the task you answered in question 1 during the period you answered in question 2.

Fact-check

1. Knowing when – what time of day and which day(s) of the week – you work best is:
   a) very helpful ❏
   b) futile and unproductive ❏
   c) useful if you have the time to think about it ❏
   d) so useful that it will be forgotten immediately ❏

2. During the time when you work best, you should:
   a) complete the small routine tasks to get them out of the way first ❏
   b) make sure it is always full of meetings ❏
   c) check your emails constantly ❏
   d) deal with the most difficult task or the one you least want to do ❏

3. At work, you should aim to:
   a) check your social media websites constantly ❏
   b) complete the small routine tasks to get them out of the way first ❏
   c) tackle the most difficult task or the one that you least want to do before dealing with less important tasks ❏
   d) spend you whole day filling in your time sheet ❏

4. When you are working on your one main task, you should:
   a) allow yourself to be distracted ❏
   b) switch off your emails and your mobile phone so that you can concentrate ❏
   c) ask your colleagues to interrupt you every ten minutes ❏
   d) check your text messages and emails every two minutes ❏

5. Building up momentum by tackling one task at a time is:
   a) helpful, as you achieve more ❏
   b) a waste of time ❏
   c) completely unrealistic ❏
   d) helpful if you have the time ❏

6. At the end of a time of creative thinking, you should:
   a) forget all your discussions as if they never happened ❏
   b) move on to the next task ❏
   c) reward yourself ❏
   d) plan the next step you need to make to put your thoughts into action ❏

7. At work, you need more time to:
   a) eat ❏
   b) think ❏
   c) socialize with colleagues ❏
   d) have business meetings ❏

8. In a SWOT analysis, SWOT stands for:
a) storms, welcome, offices, trouble ❏
b) study, work, opportunities, time ❏
c) strengths, weaknesses, opportunities, threats ❏
d) steps, wisdom, output, thinking ❏

9. Giving your mind more 'breathing space':
a) is a great idea in theory, but impractical ❏
b) makes you fall sleep very quickly ❏
c) allows time for you to come up with fresh ideas ❏
d) is a great idea for when on holiday ❏

10. Coaching or mentoring can help you:
a) avoid the real work ❏
b) think about your skills and future career ❏
c) complain about everyone and everything ❏
d) become arrogant ❏

TUESDAY

Manage your time effectively

Introduction

Today we move on to practicalities and consider:

- Clarifying your job in terms of priorities
- Distinguishing between what is urgent and what is important
- Making the most effective use of your time
- Things to do while commuting
- Keys to successful meetings
- Planning and allowing for contingencies
- Dealing with interruptions
- Delegating tasks
- Working out how much you cost your organization
- Using a diary and to-do list
- Dealing with things that waste your time
- Dealing with procrastination
- Using office technology effectively

Clarify your job

Set priorities

> *'No amount of "tricks of the trade" will avoid the need to set some sort of priority when allocating one's time.'*
>
> Sir John Harvey-Jones (1924–2008), former chairman of ICI

1 Take a piece of paper or open up a new document on your computer and write in the middle of the page what your job role is in six words. Around that role, list the tasks – the various parts of your job (what you actually do) – under different headings. Now look at that paper.

2 Write A, B, C, or D alongside each task that you do:
   A: for tasks that are important and urgent, e.g. dealing with crises
   B: for tasks that are important but not urgent, e.g. undertaking forward planning and building relationships
   C: for tasks that are not important but urgent, e.g. dealing with interruptions to your work
   D: for tasks that are neither important nor urgent, e.g. checking social media websites

A Important and urgent	B Important but not urgent
C Not important but urgent	D Not important and not urgent

3 Count up how many As, Bs, Cs and Ds you have:
   As:
   Bs:
   Cs:
   Ds:

Which category of your work has the highest rating: A, B, C or D? Now think which category most of your work should be in. The answer is B: tasks that are important but not urgent should occupy as much of your time at work as possible.

4 Now go through your tasks again. Look at the As: what practical steps can you take to turn the As into Bs? You may need to work with colleagues on this.

For example, John's colleagues in the finance department expect him to complete a task during week 2 of each month – the busiest time every month for him – but to do it, he needs information from another department that only arrives that week. John asks his colleagues in that department to supply him with information earlier, in week 1, so that he is less stressed.

5 Set up a planning diary, either on hard copy (paper) or as a computer table or spreadsheet for each day of the week (Figure 1). If you are working on hard copy, write in pencil so that you can erase certain tasks and reassign them to other times. Put your tasks as outlined in 3 at particular times each week.

Begin with Bs, making sure that you put the difficult jobs and the jobs that you don't want to do in the time (day of the week and time of day) when you are most alert. (Look back at Chapter Two (Monday) for more information on this.) For example, if you work best in the mornings, try to undertake your core work then, e.g. from 9 am to 12 noon (as in Figure 1).

Next, look at each A. Consider if you can turn any of these into Bs (see step 4 above).

Fill in any remaining As and then Cs and lastly any relevant Ds.

6 Question whether you need to do any of the Ds at all. Are any of the Ds rather like junk mail or spam that you should not be considering at all? If so, don't waste time even thinking about them.

7 What aspects of your job recur (e.g. weekly or monthly)? Insert in the relevant cells the tasks you regularly do on those days/weeks, e.g. a regular meeting on Thursday afternoons, or John's finance work in week 2 of every month. Question whether these are the best times for you.

8 Assign some thinking time to a particular day, e.g. Friday morning (after your Thursday meeting).

9 You may discover that there is too much to fit into one week. If so, could you aim to fit in all your work over a two-week cycle rather than in one week? For example, could you hold your regular Thursday meetings only twice a month, in weeks 1 and 3 rather than every week?

10 Make sure you include preparation time in your plan. For example, if your regular meeting is on Thursdays, start your preparation on Tuesdays. (Don't start on Wednesday: a crisis might arise then and, if you become involved with that, you will not be able to do your preparation. Furthermore, beginning your preparation on Tuesday allows time for your subconscious to work to produce other thoughts – as we discussed in Chapter Two (Monday).

What we have done here is to try to stand back and manage better the time that you can control. (There will always be some time that you cannot control, e.g. if you are stuck in a traffic jam on your way to work.)

These plans can then form the basis of your diary and to-do list. Even if you don't achieve this completely every day and only for three days a week instead of five, then that may be better than you are achieving at the moment and is still a useful foundation to work from.

Use a diary and to-do list

Now we've created our diary and to-do list, here are some guidelines on how to use them:

● It doesn't matter whether you have an electronic or paper diary/to-do list, as long as you have one

Figure 1 Weekly plan

	Monday	Tuesday	Wednesday	Thursday	Friday
8 am					
9 am	Core work	Core work	Core work	Core work	Thinking time
10 am	Core work	Core work	Core work	Core work	Core work
11 am	Core work	Core work	Core work	Core work	Core work
12 noon					
1 pm					
2 pm				Team meeting	
3 pm		Prepare for Thurs Team meeting			
4 pm					
5 pm					
6 pm					

- Work out your own preference: have one that you can carry with you everywhere
- Put all your key activities in your diary
- List all regular activities, e.g. any meetings that recur, for example 'first Tuesday of the month'. Do not rely on your memory for these. If you have not entered them in your diary, when a colleague phones to ask if you are free at that time, you may say yes, having forgotten you have a regular meeting. I personally have an A4-week-to-view hard copy book, in which I list all my key activities
- Use your diary as a basis for planning your to-do list. Compile your to-do list at the end of the previous day (if you leave it to the start of a new day, you will waste precious time). Tick off, cross out or delete items as you complete them
- At the end of the week, list the key activities you want to complete the following week
- If you don't complete items on one day, move them to the next

- Regularly check your to-do list during the day to make sure you are on track. (For some time, I didn't bother to do this, and found that I didn't complete tasks on the list, so it is worth doing)
- Order your items to ensure you tackle the hardest/most difficult/the ones you least want to do sooner rather than later

Make the most effective use of your time

Dealing with a few major issues has greater value than dealing with lots of minor ones. For example, 80% of the difficulties you face at work may come from three major issues and 20% from ten minor issues. This ratio is known as the *Pareto Principle*, or the 80:20 rule.[3] It is a more effective use of your time if you concentrate on the few major issues that lead to 80% of the difficulties than become preoccupied with the many issues caused by the 20%.

Work well

Here are some tips to work well and become more efficient:
- Get something right first time. Having to redo work you did not do well first time around takes more time: not only do you have to take time to find the parts that have been done poorly and then correct them, you also have to deal with any effects the bad work caused, e.g. loss of credibility or damaged reputation

> *'The best preparation for good work tomorrow is to do good work today.'*
> Elbert (Green) Hubbard (1856–1915), American
> businessman, writer, and printer

[3] The *Pareto Principle is* named after the Italian economist and sociologist, Vilfredo Frederico Pareto (1842–1923).

- Before you take a break, write down the next two or three things to do after the break. Also, if thoughts occur to you at times of day when you are not working, note them on your phone or write them down physically (I keep a notepad by the side of my bed to jot down such thoughts)
- If you can, say no to more non-relevant work, (see Chapter Seven: Saturday)

Things to do while commuting

One way to make better use of time is to use your commute effectively. Here are some suggestions of what you can do. Some of these ideas are clearly more suitable for travelling by train, others for driving.

Reading

- Reading the newspaper or a magazine
- Catching up on emails
- Reading background material
- Reading something completely unrelated to your work

Listening

- Listening to music
- Listening to the radio
- Listening to an audio book
- Listening to, and learning, a new language

Playing

- Playing games and puzzles

Sleeping

- Catching up on sleep

Watching

- Watching a video

Thinking

- Preparing for the day ahead or reviewing how the day has gone
- Thinking how to tackle difficulties

- Preparing for a presentation or difficult conversation
- Working out what to eat at home

Of course, there are many other things that you can do whilst commuting to work. How about being mindful of the drive/train ride in and enjoying the 'now'. This is a good technique to give the brain time to think.

Keys to successful meetings

For meetings to be effective, you need to:

- Know the purpose of the meeting
- Prepare for the meeting
- Keep meetings as short and as focused as possible
- Make sure that actions are well written up so that individuals know clearly what actions to take and by when

Plan a task

Planning is essential to working effectively and making good use of your time. The key elements of planning are:

- Breaking down a large task into its constituent parts
- Knowing your outcomes: what you want to achieve
- Knowing your deadline
- Knowing your resources, e.g. in terms of personnel and finance

If you do not know how long a particular task will take, don't guess by plucking a figure out of the air, but work on a sample and use that as a basis. For example, I once thought that checking 100 items in a reference book would take me a maximum of three hours. However, when I undertook a sample for half an hour, I discovered that I only completed three, and each one had taken me an average of ten minutes. 100 x ten mins = 1,000 mins = 16.7 hours, which is considerably longer than the three I originally thought.

Note that you will come up with various reasons why you were slow, for example you were learning what you have to do and you were interrupted. These might be true, and you will probably increase momentum as you work on a task, so the overall time might come down to say 12 or 13 hours, but this is still considerably higher than the original estimate of three hours.

When planning, note that the time spent undertaking admin (e.g. commissioning, checking, preparation, participation, and follow up of meetings) is likely to be far more than you think.

 TIP *When planning, the time spent doing admin is likely to be far more than you think.*

In planning schedules, remember to allow for:

- Holidays, both by individuals and public holidays
- Other work that individuals might undertake at the same time. For example, a colleague might be compiling a report for another department on the days you have allocated for him or her to be available for your project
- Unproductive time. You may sit at your desk from 9 am to 5 pm with a break for lunch, but how much of that time is actually productive? Maybe five hours
- Contingencies. Unplanned events that could significantly delay your projects. Allow 10–20% of the time as contingency

Deal with interruptions

Do all you can to minimize interruptions and build up momentum in your work. To illustrate this, consider two trains travelling along the same track to London, each covering 90 kilometres. One is non-stop and takes only 55 minutes; the other stops six times and takes 95 minutes. Ask yourself which train your work is more like: the fast or slow train? The more you can minimize interruptions, the more you will achieve. Furthermore, as you build up momentum, you will become increasingly absorbed in your task as you focus on it and your work will flow more easily.

- As far as possible, take control. Arrange meetings that fit best with your schedule, not other people's
- If someone phones you at an inconvenient time, ask them to call back at a certain time that is convenient to you. Don't say, 'I'll ring you back' – that means you will have to add them to your to-do list, which is probably too full already. Give your caller the responsibility to call you back
- Not all interruptions come from others: we sometimes interrupt ourselves by checking our emails constantly and responding to them immediately. (It may only take you a minute to answer an email but you will lose several minutes' concentration.) Schedule in regular times to check emails
- Delegate more, ensuring you give clear instructions. Train colleagues up so you can delegate more

Delegation

There are many reasons why managers don't delegate: you think you can do it better yourself; members of the team are too busy; the task is too urgent; your colleagues aren't quite ready to take on such demanding work... Most of these reasons are essentially about the fact that you don't trust members of your team to carry out the tasks. But when will they be fully ready? When will they have enough time?

You need to settle on three important ideas:

- **Plan ahead as much as you can**. Spend time doing this. You know when key tasks (e.g. the annual budget) are required. Schedule in sufficient planning time in your diary
- **Delegate work to those who are nearly ready** to receive it. No-one will ever be fully ready – were you? The delegated tasks will stretch those who are nearly ready for them. And that's what you want, isn't it?
- **Delegate more rather than less**. There are a few matters you cannot delegate (e.g. managing the overall team, allocating financial resources, dealing with confidential matters of performance management and promotion), but you can and should delegate many of your tasks and some routine administration

How to delegate

- Know your team. Who would be the best person to carry out the tasks you want to delegate? Remember what I just noted: choose colleagues who are nearly ready. If no-one is at that level, then provide some training so that at least some of them are. Share the load wherever possible, but don't delegate too much work to your best colleague
- Be clear about the tasks you want to delegate. This is the most important part of delegating. Don't give vague instructions (e.g. 'Could you just write a short report on failings in security?'), but be specific. Explain yourself well ('I'd like a 10-page report giving examples of major security breaches, together with possible reasons behind them and recommendations on how to avoid them in future.') Allow plenty of time to explain the task and give an opportunity for your colleague to ask you questions so they can clarify what you want them to do
- Check that they have understood the task you want them to undertake. Don't do this by just asking, 'Have you understood what I want you to do?' but phrase the question to be something like 'Could you summarize what you will be doing?' Their response will show how much they have understood your explanation
- Give sufficient significant background details so that your colleague knows why they are doing the task and where their task or activity fits into the overall scheme of things
- Where possible, follow up any spoken instructions in writing with a full brief, outlining the work
- Break the task or activity down into its constituent parts. Write briefing instructions, but don't just write in abstract terms: give examples of what needs to be done
- State the date and time you want your colleague to complete the work by. Remember that what may take you (with all your experience) only half a day will probably take the colleague you are delegating the task to much longer, e.g. two days
- Agree how often you want them to report back to you, particularly (but not only) when they have completed certain agreed targets

- If a colleague is slow at doing his or her work, ask them to give you an update on their progress by the end of each day
- Be clear about the authority and responsibility you are giving your colleague with this work. After all, you remain ultimately responsible as manager, even though you have delegated the work
- Provide the necessary equipment and other resources (and if necessary further training) that they need
- Let them decide the details of how they will undertake the work
- Where problems or difficulties arise, encourage your colleague to come to you about them, but also to bring their own thoughts on possible solutions, together with (for example) any figures on financial costings for such solutions and the time implementing them would take. This makes better use of your time: they are closer to the details of the task than you are. Your task is then to make a decision based on the suggestions. Getting your colleague to think things through for themselves also increases their skills
- When they have completed the task, thank your colleague, expressing your appreciation. Recognize them and their achievement

---

Working out how much you cost your organization

It isn't just you who needs to worry about your productivity and efficiency as a leader. Everything you do at work has an impact on your organization too. The less efficient an employee is, the more it costs.

If you have an annual salary of £30,000

÷ 48 (52 weeks – 4 weeks holiday) = £625 per week

÷ 5 (days per week) = £125 per day

÷ 5 (productive hours in that day; could be as low as 2!) = £25

× 2.7 per hour (to cover office overheads) = £67.50

So the cost of five managers attending a meeting lasting seven hours would be £2,363 (67.5 x 5 x 7), *which is probably higher than you thought.*

Note these figures are what you cost your company – not what you earn.

Twenty things that can waste your time ... and your response to them

1 Saying 'I'll just finish these small tasks first' but never starting your main task seriously. Response: start your major task first whether you feel like it or not.
2 Indecision by managers. Response: remember that making no decision is also a decision in itself. Be courageous and either make a decision, or encourage a decision to be made. Make sure that SMART actions are agreed.
3 Poor internal communications (e.g. with your boss). Response: discuss the issues with them (see also Chapter Six: Friday).
4 Your own perfectionism. Response: do less! You don't need to triple-check every cell in a spreadsheet in which the numbers have been computer generated
5 Lack of concentration. Response: motivate yourself – promise yourself a reward upon completion within a certain time.
6 Fear of getting something wrong. Response: ask for help; go on a training course. Ask for feedback.
7 Surfing the Internet for social networking purposes. Response: be stricter with yourself. Avoid non-work internet until lunchtime.
8 Colleagues needing help. Response: ensure you help them in your less than prime time, if possible. Schedule them in so they know you will do it.
9 Someone who just wants to chat. Response: talk during lunch or after work.
10 Panicking colleagues. Response: tell them you will help them this time but not in future. Don't allow responding to others' crises become a regular occurance.
11 Other colleagues constantly interrupting. Response: schedule and make known the specific times when you are available.
12 Looking for things. Response: store or file items more sensibly; throw more things away.

13 Phone calls. Response: turn off your mobile during prime time; screen other calls. Ask the caller to call back at a specific time.

14 Having things you need far away from you. Response: move them closer; get organized.

15 A growing to-do list. Response: prioritize items:
   - Put one star beside unimportant matters
   - Put two stars beside important matters
   - Put three stars beside important and urgent matters
   - Do the three-star items first: now

16 Not knowing where to start in a task. Response: break a larger task down into smaller steps. If necessary, just start somewhere.

17 Constantly thinking of new ways of doing tasks that have been done many times before. Response: for tasks that recur, create templates and file them where you know where they are.

18 Hesitating about over what to write. Response: write something or draw a mind map Ask yourself the question words *who*, *why*, *what*, *when, how*, *where, which*? to set yourself thinking. You can always go back and edit it later.

19 Answering emails all the time. Response: set certain times when you will check and answer them.

20 Trying to do too many different things. Response: Constantly opening and closing computer files takes time in itself; you will build up momentum if you do fewer tasks well. Use your star list (see 15).

Five steps to deal with procrastination

Procrastination is postponing things you need to do until later (*cras* is Latin for 'tomorrow'). You can spend a lot of time being very busy, but not actually work on the jobs that need doing.

1 Focus on the result, not the activity. Set yourself a target of what you can achieve in ten minutes. Then, after that ten minutes, set yourself another target of what you can achieve in the next ten minutes and so on.

2 Make yourself plan better in future – use that diary and to-do list.

3 Break down a big task into smaller, manageable chunks. Take one step at a time, however small.

4 Ask for help from others, but don't use your fear of failure as an excuse for doing nothing. Do something: even write an outline, which can then be a basis for developing further ideas.

5 Don't wait until you feel motivated or you will wait forever. For more on motivating yourself, see Chapter Five (Thursday). Do one small step now.

Five principles of effective time management

1 Know what time of day and day(s) of the week you work best and protect that time. Use it for thinking/hard tasks – e.g. no emails!

2 Tackle the hardest task – the thing you don't want to do – first.

3 Handle pieces of paper/complete a task at one sitting. Handle a piece of paper only once. To see if you are doing that, put a red dot at the top right-hand side of a piece of paper every time you handle it. When you have finished the task, you should only have one red dot on each piece of paper.

4 Use slack time well, e.g. for writing, reading, making a phone call, filing (electronic or manual), clearing your in-tray, reading a periodical.

5 If you have 30 minutes available for a task, aim to fit in a task that might take at least that amount rather than one that will only last 20 minutes, leaving you spare time.

Remember 3Ds: do – dump – delegate: .

Do -	deal with it. If you need to do it, think: • how long something will take. If it will take literally between 30 seconds and 2 minutes, then do it now • if it is urgent and important, start it now • if it is less urgent, or will take more than 2 minutes, then defer it by planning when you will do it, depending on how important it is
Dump -	If you don't need it, and it's not important, get rid of it – throw it away. You can recycle non-confidential paper, but you should make sure you shred papers that are confidential
Delegate -	pass it on to someone else.

'Work expands so as to fill the time available for its completion.'

– 'Parkinson's Law', named after the English historian and journalist Cyril Northolt Parkinson (1909–93).

To make good use of your time, use office technology effectively

- Use Outlook; share files online; arrange invitations to meetings automatically; flag emails to follow up so they don't get lost
- Synchronize electronic/digital devices; use Dropbox to share documents; cloud computing; coordinate calendar and contacts
- Create more templates and checklists so you don't have to repeat the same work each time
- Use speed-dial on the phone; list of contacts
- Use predictive text

Certain software packages offer other time-saving devices:

- Use 'track changes' to note changes that colleagues make to documents
- Use templates; create macros
- File material under names you can remember and would be intuitive to colleagues in your absence. Or better still, agree standard formats for filenames
- Use shortcuts, for example:
  - shift F3 to change capitals
  - shift F7 for a substantial thesaurus
- Use automatic reminders, e.g. for birthdays
- Use 'autocorrect' for words that you type often. This is the facility that is preloaded onto your computer and automatically changes, for example, 'freind' to 'friend'. So if you are often typing the name of your company 'Kramer Consultants', you can set up your computer so that every time you type 'KC1' (for example) it is automatically changed to 'Kramer Consultants'. Look up 'autocorrect' under 'Help' to find out how to set it up; it isn't difficult and it will save you a lot of time

Look under the 'Help' function of your computer programmes to learn how to use these shortcuts. A small amount of time invested now can save hours later on.

Summary

Someone who manages their time well will:

- Plan well
- Know when they work best
- Meet schedules and deadlines
- Concentrate on priorities
- Participate effectively in meetings
- Create 'blocks of time', e.g. to check emails or make routine phone calls.
- Handle interruptions well
- Be organized
- Delegate when possible
- Make good use of meetings
- Use slack time well

Exercise

1 List the tasks that you do at your work and try to move as many urgent and important ones ('As') to important but not urgent ones ('Bs').

2 Compile a weekly plan of the tasks you do, using the principles outlined today.

3 Think of a schedule that you are compiling: make sure you have included some contingency time.

Fact-check

1. As regards priorities:
   a) I've no idea what the priorities of my job are ❏
   b) I know what my priorities are and stick to them most of the time ❏
   c) I set priorities but never stick to them ❏
   d) I'm so concerned with the urgent that I never consider priorities ❏

2. When thinking about my job, I need mostly to do:
   a) tasks that are not important but urgent ❏
   b) tasks that are neither important nor urgent ❏
   c) tasks that are important and urgent ❏
   d) tasks that are important but not urgent ❏

3. I get side-tracked by unimportant parts of my job:
   a) all the time ❏
   b) rarely ❏
   c) most days ❏
   d) never ❏

4. I plan my time:
   a) never ❏
   b) occasionally in my head ❏
   c) nearly always ❏
   d) I've no time to do that ❏

5. I have a work diary:
   a) but never use it ❏
   b) and am a slave to it ❏
   c) and use it nearly all the time to plan ❏
   d) I've no time to do that ❏

6. I write a to-do list:
   a) what's that? ❏
   b) and am a slave to it ❏
   c) and keep to it as far as I can ❏
   d) but never look at it during the day ❏

7. When I compile a schedule, I allow time for contingency:
   a) always ❏
   b) never ❏
   c) when I remember ❏
   d) what is 'contingency'? ❏

8. I check my emails:
   a) 24 hours a day ❏
   b) all the time during the working day ❏
   c) when I come back from holiday ❏
   d) at regular times through the working day ❏

9. I delegate:
   a) tasks to colleagues who I want to develop ❏
   b) badly ❏
   c) the tasks I don't want to do ❏
   d) never ❏

10. I wait until I feel motivated before I start work:
    a) always ❏
    b) never: I push myself to do something even if I don't feel like it ❏
    c) usually ❏
    d) occasionally ❏

WEDNESDAY

Manage your mind decisively

Introduction

So far this week, we've looked generally at becoming aware of what kind of person you are – your skills, values, motives, beliefs, attitudes – and then we looked at managing your focus: keeping the main thing the main thing and not being distracted. We also considered it important to have 'free' time so that you can have some 'breathing space', and then yesterday we considered managing your time better.

We now turn to managing your mind and thoughts. Today we will look at:

- Thinking positive thoughts
- Developing ways of thinking
- Looking at the example of different aspects of decision making: defining your aims, collecting relevant information, identifying different options, considering risks and consequences, and making and implementing the decision
- The role of intuition
- Solving problems
- Challenging assumptions and being imaginative
- Ways to remember things
- Reading more effectively

Think positive thoughts

'Nurture your mind with great thoughts, for you will never go any higher than you think.'

Benjamin Disraeli (1804–81), English statesman, prime minister and novelist

Our mind is the base of our reason and decision making. Just as we are encouraged to watch what we eat in order to maintain a healthy lifestyle physically, so we also need to be alert to what we take into our minds. That will strengthen us and help us respond positively to negative things around us.

What we take into our minds affects what flows out of us. Therefore, we need to guard what we take into our minds and be careful what we look at and read. We need to keep up-to-date with the news, and also with trends in our industry and useful aspects of business thinking (see the resources in Seven 7s at the end of this book). We also need positive input into our minds to counteract the negative things that we constantly face.

It is also good to stretch our minds and discuss matters with people we disagree with. They might be right, and even if they are not we will have refined our own understanding.

Develop your thoughts

When I am faced with a task that needs thought, I draw a pattern diagram (also known as a mind map). This is a very useful way of opening up a subject. In a group setting, 'brainstorming' is a similar tool.

Take a blank piece of A4 paper. Arrange it in landscape position and write the subject that you are considering in the middle. (Write a word or few words, but not a whole sentence.) You may find it helpful to work in pencil, as you can rub out what you write if necessary.

Now, towards the edge of the paper, write around your central word(s) the different key aspects that come to your mind. You do not need to list ideas in order of importance;

simply write them down. To begin with, you do not need to join the ideas up with lines linking connected items.

If you get stuck at any point, ask yourself the questions *why*, *how*, *what*, *who*, *when*, *where*, *how much* and *how many*. These may well set you thinking.

When I do this, I am often amazed at: (1) how easy the task is: it doesn't feel like work! The ideas and concepts seem to flow naturally and spontaneously. (2) how valuable that piece of paper is. I have captured all (or at least some or many) of the key points. I don't want to lose that piece of paper!

An example of a pattern diagram for the subject of buying a new computer system is:

Users
- Which company departments will use the system?

Cost
- Budget
- Check figures with Finance Director

IT department
- Who will build the new system?
- Who will install the new system?

Website maintenance

Locations
- On company's two sites

Time available
- Should be ready for 1 Jan

New computer system

Old system
- Keeps crashing
- Secure?
- Software: Out of date
- Slow, constant problems

Kinds of computers
- Laptops
- iPads
- Latest technology
- How long is it intended to last?

Accounts department
- Will they move over to new system?
- They introduced a new system only 6 months ago

Link to Intranet

Security

Think creatively

Other ways to encourage you to think creatively

1 Turn the subject on its head: for example, rather than thinking of ways to improve customer service in a restaurant, think of the factors that would make the customer service in that restaurant the worst in the city – e.g. no-one greets you, you have to wait a long time before ordering, the food, when it eventually arrives, is tasteless, etc.

2 Imagine yourself in a successful situation: how would you feel?

3 Pick a concrete noun and see how the problem you are trying to define is different from that.

4 Do word association: e.g. if something has a high quality, ask yourself and others what associated words that raises in your mind? Best? Expensive? Prestigious?

5 Draw the problem that is facing you: what colour is it; what shape? Or act it out as a play.

6 Consider your problem as a metaphor: a journey as a ship's voyage; a company working together as a team; increasing sales as climbing a mountain; new life as blossom on a tree. What do these fresh ways of thinking suggest?

See also Chapter Two (Monday).

Decision making

Let's take an example of developing thoughts in terms of decision making. We can list the various steps in making a decision:

Define your aims clearly

You need to identify:

- What is the real issue that you need to make a decision about and what are secondary issues?
- The time when the decision has to be made by. Is that timescale realistic? If not, can you work out a strategy to find more time?
- What kind of person you are, especially as regards your values, what motivates you at work and what is the way in which you work?
- What your personality is as regards decision making: e.g. are you naturally decisive or indecisive, or are you cautious or rash?
- Who in your company or organization makes the decisions. Is it only you as manager, or do you involve others? When a decision is made that affects colleagues, the greater the

involvement of colleagues in the decision-making process, the stronger their motivation
- Who will implement the decision?

Collect relevant information

As regards the decision you need to make, you need to:

- Understand the context
- Gather relevant information, including consulting experts as necessary
- Work on your costs and schedules for implementing the decision

Identify different options

When you consider a range of techniques to help you identify different options in your decision making, you should:

- Consider imaginative alternatives: widen your thinking so that you don't stick with what you are used to and don't choose the first option that offers itself
- Challenge assumptions; see also later today
- Consider where you can concentrate your resources so that they are used most effectively
- Consider the timing: work out which tasks need to be done before others can be started
- Examine a situation carefully before 'jumping to conclusions'. If you are a negative person by temperament, don't give up but always look at the options and manage your way through them

Consider risks

Assessing risk means knowing how and when things could go wrong and working out ways to deal with them. It is important to manage risks so that the threats of possible risks are minimized. For example, if you are making decisions about managing a project, risks are the uncertain events that could happen which would prevent your project from being carried out successfully. Is the schedule realistic? Have sufficient financial resources been made available? Are roles and responsibilities clear? Are you measuring the quality of what you are producing objectively enough? Have you allowed for contingency in your schedule and costings?

Risks need to be identified, assessed and then dealt with. The one key point to remember is that you will not survive in business without encountering certain risks, so it is better to plan to deal with them rather than be surprised when they unexpectedly arise.

Consider the consequences

Every decision has consequences, but your task as manager is to:

- Be aware of the consequences of choosing different options
- Evaluate the consequences of choosing different options
- Minimize the risks of choosing different options

To do this, you need to do more than just imagine that you might choose a particular option. You need to actually think what would happen if you did choose it. Be both subjective (e.g. what would it feel like?) and objective (e.g. what would be the profit or loss?). Use criteria that are in line with the values you and/or your company or organization hold.

Here you deliberately think of:

- What would happen if you did nothing? Sometimes this is a valid option. Sometimes the response to a crisis (not always!) can be to continue as if nothing has happened and the crisis might exhaust itself and fade away
- What would happen if the decision was not made *now*? Can you delay it?
- What would happen if the decision was not made *by you*? Is it your decision to make – or is it the responsibility of you and others?
- What would happen if you adopted each of the options that emerge? You need to do this *before* you make your choice.

For example, when preparing for negotiations, consider whether agreeing to deliver the products within three months is a realistic schedule for you. If it is not, don't offer it in the first place

● What possible future situations could develop

Don't ignore your intuition

'I just know', 'I felt that was right', 'I had a hunch that ...', 'The thought just came to me'. How often do you use or hear such phrases? Intuition has a role to play in the decision-making process.

It can be defined as 'the power of knowing something without evident reasoning'. There may be no logical explanation for something; you discern the truth about a person or situation and you just know it is right.

For me, intuition is important, but it is only one factor in the decision-making process. If I am tired or stressed, my emotions can play havoc with my thinking processes, so I have to be careful.

Intuition is linked to your depth mind, your subconscious, as we discussed in Chapter Two (Monday). It seems that your depth mind digests a myriad of thoughts – analysing, synthesizing and evaluating them – resulting in an intuitive thought coming to your consciousness.

That is why it is useful to 'sleep on it': sleep for a night before making a significant decision. Sometimes this is plain common sense. I have an informal rule for myself that I do not send out a costing for a project without sleeping on it. A while back, I costed a project one day and, when I checked my figures the next day, I realized I had for some inexplicable reason calculated the figure to be only half the correct total. So there is ordinary wisdom as well as intuitive reason behind the need to 'sleep on it'. Don't ignore the thoughts that occur to you when you are taking a shower or driving home from work and are not thinking about a problem. Allow your subconscious mind the opportunity to do its work and let fresh ideas emerge when you are not thinking about making the decision.

Evaluate the different options

Having too many options can be overwhelming and lead to confusion, which can also add time to the decision making. To be more efficient, evaluate your options and see which ones can be eliminated. You should:

- Reduce the number of options available, to enable you to make a decision
- Establish certain objective criteria against which you can assess each of your different options
- Consider the consequences of each option and their advantages and disadvantages. You may need to make a compromise
- List the resources needed to fulfil each option, e.g. costing
- Assess risks: knowing how and when things could go wrong, and therefore being prepared for them

Make the decision

You will eventually arrive at the point of coming to a decision. Having defined the core issues, gathered information, identified and evaluated the various options, and weighed up each of the options in your mind, you now need to make the decision. Next, you need to implement it, communicate it to all the relevant colleagues and, if necessary, set in place good monitoring controls to help you track progress.

Solve problems

Here are some guidelines to help you find a satisfactory way of dealing with a problem or difficulty:

- Ask if it is your problem. Is it your responsibility to respond to it? Is it someone else's? Or is it just one of those things you have to live with? If the problem is yours:
- how important is it? Will solving it have a significant effect on your work?

- how urgent is it? If the problem will become more serious if you do nothing about it, then act sooner rather than later *Occasionally, however, some problems can turn into positive opportunities, so don't always think you have to solve them all*
- Get to the root of the problem. Think; discuss with other colleagues; analyse the problem by separating it into its parts to help you define it more closely and understand it more fully
- In particular, concentrate on the causes – not the symptoms or effects – of the problem. So if someone's work is below standard, don't keep on moaning about it by giving examples but try to find out why and ask whether they need training, or whether they would be more suitable for other kinds of work
- Keep on asking questions, especially the question 'Why?' so that you gain a complete understanding of the real issue. Problem solving is often more about asking the right questions than giving the right answers
- Gather information as to the extent of the problem. If the quality of products is failing, does this affect 1 in 1,000 products or 900 in 1,000?
- Concentrate on the big issues. Don't get bogged down in detail
- Use your experience. As you progress as a manager, you will develop that sense of 'I've been here before – how did I solve the problem last time?' Use your colleagues' experience: how did they solve a similar problem?
- Consider different responses. Here are some techniques you could use to respond creatively to problems:
  - Brainstorm with colleagues: take a flipchart. Ask one person to state the problem and then get him or her to write down ideas as the problem is thought about and discussed from different angles, e.g. what would your customers' and your competitors' viewpoint be? Encourage the participants to build on one another's ideas; don't criticize or evaluate them. At the end, participants can agree how to take the best ideas to the next stage

- Draw up a flow chart that shows the series of steps of all the different stages that led to a problem, how the problem is expressed (i.e. its symptoms) and the connections between the problem's causes and effects
- Think 'outside the box'. Is the problem difficult to put into words? Then draw it or work out if you are better explaining it by a painting, in a piece of music or by role play
- Draw a pattern diagram (see earlier today)
- Conduct a SWOT analysis (see Chapter Two: Monday).

Challenge assumptions

When you are generating ideas and coming up with estimates, challenge the assumptions you make.

- Be prepared to think differently, e.g. be explicit if your present strategy is failing. Face up to the 'elephant in the room', the subject everyone is aware of but is not discussed because it is too uncomfortable
- Are you keeping up with (if not acting in advance of) trends in your industry?
- Don't be overcautious

Develop your memory

Developing your memory is one of the skills that will help you become a more effective manager. It will train your mind and deepen your understanding.

When meeting someone for the first time, concentrate particularly: think hard as the other person says their name. If appropriate, write it down as soon as you can. If you are not sure of the spelling, ask and or write down some phonetic version of the name. Using their name when talking to them sometimes will help reinforce the memory of their name in your mind.

Try to establish some association between what you are trying to remember and something you already know, e.g. a woman's name Daphne and the visual association of a daffodil: maybe she is wearing a yellow ribbon or dress.

Develop a set of initial letters to remember a list of things: I do this quite often if I am shopping, e.g. for toothpaste, milk and a newspaper: TMN. I may remember a sentence, ToMorrow's Newspaper, to remind me, or a picture of someone sitting in an armchair reading a newspaper with some toothpaste on the arm of the chair. The more unusual the picture, the more memorable it will be.

Read more effectively

As a manager you will have a lot of material to read – for example, emails, reports, websites, professional literature, contracts, technical manuals, etc.

Here are some guidelines to help you read more effectively:

- Decide on your aims in reading a particular text. Do you want to simply check a fact, gain an overall sense of a text, grasp a detailed knowledge of a subject (for example for a report or presentation you have to prepare) or evaluate the writer's arguments and views?
- Vary the speed at which you read a text, depending on the kind of text you are reading. Spend more time on important and/or difficult parts of the text and less time on less important and/or easier parts
- Try not to mouth words as you read them. Mouthing words in this way not only slows you down but also means that you focus on the words rather than their meaning
- Put your finger immediately to the right of the first word on the paper/screen and move your finger across the line of words at a speed that your eyes can keep up with. You will find that your finger gently 'pulls' you along at a faster rate than your normal reading speed. Alternatively, put your finger on the paper/screen and move your finger down the page at a speed that your eyes can keep up with, reading just above it
- For some important work, take notes of what you have read. Summarizing the author's argument in your own words can be a particularly useful tool
- If you want to undertake a more detailed read of part of a text:

- Find out which sections of the text you want to read. Consult the contents/list of chapters or index. Or if you are reading on screen, use the 'find' facility to locate the words you are most interested in. Survey or scan the text to get a wider view of it. As you do that, you will begin to see the writer's key words and phrases
- Look out for the signposts: the introduction and conclusions; the words *firstly*, *secondly*; the beginning of paragraphs; such expressions as *on the one hand* and *on the other hand*, which guide you in seeing the structure of the text and can be helpful to your understanding
- Focus on the key words and, even more importantly, key phrases
- Reword the main points in your mind, on computer or on paper. Express the author's key points in your own way. Think about the author's argument: do you agree with him/her? Does the text make assumptions that you disagree with? Ask questions of the text and see if they are answered. Engage your mind
- At the end of reading, see if you can recall the main points, or even better, see if you can explain the main points to someone else. You could even review what you have read later to check that you still recall it

Effective reading ... and good time management

As a manager, Sarah was methodical about her reading. She only checked her emails a few times a day, dealing with essential matters as they arose. She didn't bother to check the many junk emails she received, but simply deleted them.

Sarah allocated Friday mornings, when she knew she generally received fewer emails, to important but not urgent reading material that enabled her to do her job more effectively.

As she was preparing to relax for the weekend on Friday afternoons, she read non-urgent but useful material that kept her up-to-date with other trends in the industry, which were not directly related to her job but developed her wider professional knowledge.

Of course, sometimes very urgent matters arose which meant that she could not always keep to this methodical time allocation, so in such cases she was flexible. Generally, however, Sarah was able to allot sufficient resources of time to reading what was useful and essential, and to manage her time well.

Summary

Today we have considered your mind and thoughts in practical terms, especially in the context of decision making, creative thinking and problem solving. Things to be aware of include:

- how you think and feel
- how good your memory is
- effective reading
- what your time management is like

Exercise

1 Do you take time to think? Are your thoughts positive? How can you make them even more positive?

2 Draw a pattern diagram for a subject you are thinking about or have to write a report on.

3 Which step in decision making do you need to work more effectively at?

- Defining your aims
- Collecting relevant information
- Identifying different options
- Considering risks and consequences
- Making the decision
- Implementing and communicating the decision
- Tracking and monitoring progress

4 What method could you use to remember things, e.g. people's names, better?

5 Which point about reading was particularly new to you that you will put into practice? When is the next opportunity for you to do this?

SUNDAY

MONDAY

TUESDAY

WEDNESDAY

THURSDAY

FRIDAY

SATURDAY

Fact-check

1. Thinking is:
a) a luxury these days ❑
b) a waste of time ❑
c) important, to be an effective manager ❑
d) useful if you have the time ❑

2. Thinking positively is:
a) useful if you have the time ❑
b) necessary to rise above the problems of life ❑
c) too idealistic ❑
d) a stupid idea ❑

3. A pattern diagram is a useful way:
a) to start to tackle different aspects of a subject ❑
b) just to draw lines on a page ❑
c) of spending ten minutes ❑
d) what is a pattern diagram anyway? ❑

4. When making a decision:
a) I just guess ❑
b) I think of a number and double it ❑
c) I look at all the different options but never actually make a decision ❑
c) I identify the issue, collect information and evaluate the different options ❑

5. Considering risks and consequences is:
a) important ❑
b) a luxury in this fast-paced world ❑
c) a waste of time ❑
d) useful, if you remember ❑

6. Your intuition is:
a) always an infallible guide ❑
b) one factor in the decision-making process ❑
c) unreal ❑
d) never something you should consider ❑

7. When solving a problem, it is necessary to:
a) blame the person whose fault it is ❑
b) get to the root of the problem ❑
c) spend all the time thinking about minor details ❑
d) pass the responsibility of solving it back to your boss ❑

8. Challenging assumptions:
a) is just part of your nature if you are an awkward kind of person ❑
b) always wrong ❑
c) essential to do on every occasion in life ❑
d) can sometimes be useful in leading to a fresh answer ❑

9. I have a bad memory:
a) so I can't do anything about it ❑
b) so I work to improve it ❑
c) and I've forgotten what I can do about it ❑
d) but I can still remember details of my childhood ❑

10. I read:

a) everything very slowly ❑

b) everything very quickly, not being able to recall anything I have read ❑

c) carefully and selectively, sometimes making notes or trying to express the content in my own words ❑

d) nothing, ever ❑

THURSDAY

Manage your emotions carefully

Introduction

I like trains. If I am leading a workshop or giving a presentation somewhere, I prefer travelling by train to driving my car as the train gives me time to think and read. But events do happen that are outside of our control. Twice I've been on trains that have been severely delayed because of suicides. It's interesting to see how we as passengers react. All too easily, the initial thoughts that I and my fellow passengers have are ones of anger at the inconvenience we have to suffer because of the delay. When I've found myself becoming angry, however, I have had to make myself think of the victim and their family: their experience must surely be far more intense than mine. We cannot always control what happens to us in life, but we can control our emotional response to such events.

Today, we look at the area of managing our emotions:

- Don't ignore feelings
- Recognize your own emotional make-up
- Manage your thoughts
- Challenge assumptions
- Express feelings
- Don't blame, but reframe
- Be positive, and become more resilient and confident
- Motivate yourself

Don't ignore feelings

Think of an incident in your life when something bad happened to you. For example, in one job I discovered I was being paid less than a colleague who was doing the same work and who had a similar background, skills and experience to me. The issue itself was pay, but alongside that I felt angry, undervalued and unimportant.

In other words, there is the incident itself, then, underlying, there are the emotions surrounding the incident. Sometimes, after we have dealt with the facts, the unpleasant effects from the incident remain, or as we say, 'we are left with a bad taste in our mouth'; we still have to cope with our feelings, which should not be ignored. In this case, my sense of identity was affected.

Recognize your own emotional make-up

Different cultures express emotions differently. I have some African friends and they tend to be exuberant and show their emotions quite regularly. I'm more British and I'm not very emotional. I'm normally fairly even-tempered and I rarely cry. Generally, life is a steady course but I do have emotions and these surface from time to time. I feel great sadness and anger at the many injustices in the world. I become angry when I see resources of time and money being wasted.

Looking back, my parents did not often express their feelings towards each other. We didn't generally discuss emotions as a family – what counted were events. So I am having to learn to handle that part of my life: to accept feelings as part of a natural and healthy life.

It is here that we sometimes go wrong. It is wrong to ignore our emotions. We are surrounded by the claims that 'Real men don't cry', that it is wrong to feel anger or express fears, but we cannot always have strong feelings of happiness.

So it can be helpful to think: what is your emotional make-up? What is your attitude to your emotions? Which emotions do you find easy to express? Which more difficult?

I find it helpful to write down my feelings and also explore them with my wife and some trusted friends. In that way, I can accept them, usually see their significance and can be helped to move on.

Sometimes our feelings spill over into judgments about others. For example, we may help someone a lot over many years but they never thank us. Our anger may burst out into a judgment: 'You only think about yourself all the time, never anyone else.' Note that this is different from a statement about our feelings, which might be, 'I feel hurt. I thought we were friends.'

Manage your thoughts

The way in which we can manage our feelings is to manage our thoughts. Remember that emotions are not thoughts. However, they can affect how we act.

Dealing with fear

Fear can be a stumbling block in making progress in life: fear of failure, of what might happen, of what others think of us. Fear can make us feel weak, draining our energy.

Positive ways of dealing with fear include:

● Ask yourself, 'What's the worst that can happen?' If the worst really did happen, think what you would do
● Take small steps – if you are fearful of giving a 30-minute presentation, try a three-minute one to start with, then a five-minute one, and gradually build up to 30 minutes. Begin by setting small goals. Fulfilling those will develop your confidence. Set yourself realistic expectations. When I go on a long-haul flight, I keep an eye on our progress. For example, I work out when on a 13-hour flight what percentage of the journey I have covered after say 45 minutes (6%), 1.5 hours (12%) and so on. Focusing on the end goal, dividing up the overall journey time and measuring progress in a concrete way helps me feel I am on my way to reaching the goal

- Sometimes, the fear doesn't go away: Don't wait for courage; *be* courageous. I used to think that courage is the opposite of fear, but it isn't: courage is an inner strength to *decide* to do something difficult or dangerous, even if the fears are present

- Don't be too cautious, if that is your natural tendency. I am naturally quite cautious. I remember leaving my house many years ago to go to a publishing meeting. A little voice inside me said, 'Why are you going? You know that nothing will happen.' I made myself go, however, and at the meeting we agreed to compile a book that later sold well over 80,000 copies. What if I had listened to my naturally cautious self and had not been adventurous? You can be so cautious that you never do anything. Ask yourself what have you always wanted to try? Is now the time to do it? If not now, then when?

Challenge assumptions

We have feelings, which are based on certain thoughts. These thoughts are in turn based on certain assumptions. So we may need to challenge such assumptions to see if they are really true. If they turn out to be false, we can change our thoughts.

For example, if you are having a difficult conversation with a colleague, you may make assumptions about the intentions of the other party. However, you see and hear only what a person is doing and saying, not the intentions behind what they have done or said.

In order to challenge assumptions about others' intentions, you need to uncover what their intentions are. A clear, neutral, moderate statement such as 'I realize that I don't really know how you see this matter' can be a way to open up a conversation to its next stage. By acknowledging that you do not understand someone else's intentions – and that you are committed to understanding them and their views – can be a significant step forward in encouraging a colleague to express and articulate their intentions.

Sheila was jealous

Sheila was jealous of Rosey. It seemed Rosey was always chosen to be project leader. Sheila was angry: she felt she was always being ignored when it came to being chosen to lead projects and she thought she had skills that were not being recognized. She talked things over with a close colleague, Jinju, who helped her see that she was responsible for her own feelings. Sheila's feelings were real enough, but she needed to realize she could choose how she responded to them. Sheila also came to see that the feelings she was bottling up inside her were better expressed in a safe context rather than in personal anger towards Rosey.

Over time, Sheila took responsibility for herself. She learnt to face up to her own insecurities and to become more patient with both herself and Rosey. Gradually, Sheila even began to respect Rosey's qualities as a leader, even though her style was different from Sheila's. In due course Sheila's manager felt she had grown in personal maturity so much that she was chosen to lead projects.

Express emotions

Earlier today, we discussed the need not to ignore emotions. But we need to do more than that: we need to express them. Here, I think it is helpful to see expressing feelings as one stage and solving a problem as a separate, later stage. So if someone loses their temper and is allowed to express themselves freely for a few minutes, that clears the air and then they will probably feel better. We must resist the temptation to try to stop someone in the middle of expressing their anger, but allow them to release their feelings and then move on from that.

As we allow people to air their own opinions and express deep emotions, the result can – if managed well – be that some long-standing issues can be resolved, leading to stronger, more trusting working relationships.

If you have some long-bottled up emotions within you, consider finding a trusted colleague and asking them if you could have a chat about them with the goal of releasing those feelings in the first instance, rather than trying to find solutions for them immediately.

Acknowledge the emotions
of your colleagues

After feelings have been expressed, it is important to acknowledge them, perhaps by saying, 'I didn't know you felt that way.' Acknowledging the expression of feelings is an important step because in so doing you are affirming your appreciation of the other person's feelings. For more on affirming others, see Chapter Six (Friday).

Our sense of identity

When we criticize someone, for example for the poor quality of their work, they may feel threatened and become defensive. They may start to justify themselves, reminding us of all the good aspects of their work. Moreover, when our work is criticized, it is not just our work that is affected; deep within us we feel threatened and our sense of identify may be damaged.

After giving a brief presentation a few years ago, a colleague told me my work was 'not professional'. I was surprised, hurt and confused. My self-image was challenged and my sense of self-worth was attacked.

If our identity is attacked, we feel insecure and may begin to believe what is being said about our character, skills or knowledge: 'Maybe I am no good, after all.' Here we need to think realistically about ourselves – we are neither perfect in every way nor extremely incompetent. We need to manage our thoughts (see earlier today and Chapter Four: Wednesday) and let the facts influence our thoughts.

Don't blame; reframe

During a difficult conversation with someone, it can become relatively easy to blame the other person: 'It's all your fault that the report is three days late. You should have finished it earlier.' A better way is to see what each side has contributed to the difficulty. Maybe you were slightly late in giving your colleague the figures they needed for the report. Here, it is important to be professional and assert that your aim is not to blame anyone. Instead, you want to discover what went wrong, the reasons for that and what each colleague, including yourself, can learn from it.

Reframing is changing the way someone thinks about something they perceive as difficult and negative into seeing it in a more positive manner.

I first encountered reframing when I was coaching a colleague who hated interviews. She said she did not cope at all well with one-to-ones. But she also told me she enjoyed negotiating. She relished the challenge of preparing for a negotiation, listening for clues as to the other party's intentions, discussing alternatives and reaching an agreement. So my suggestion that she should adapt and reframe her thinking and see interviews positively and as a means of negotiation was a moment of sudden enlightenment for her.

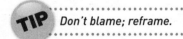

TIP *Don't blame; reframe.*

Think positively

Eddy felt frustrated. He began the job well, but soon became frustrated by the endless meetings and office politics. He started to feel trapped and could not change his situation. He could see no way out. He sat down with a friend, Ravi, and they chatted. Ravi told him to take a long look at his situation: having a job and being paid for it was better than having no job, like some of his friends from school. Eddy and Ravi discussed how there were a few positive things about his job, like the opportunities it gave him to travel to various cities and meet new people. As he thought about them he realized he was not so badly off after all.

Build up your confidence

Ways in which you can increase your confidence include:

- Prepare better. If you lack confidence at giving presentations, then work harder at your preparation. The more prepared you are, the more you will feel in control and the greater confidence you will have. You will then feel less nervous. Your preparation could include relatively simple things like dealing with practical arrangements or taking a copy of your PowerPoint presentation (saved in an earlier version of PowerPoint to be on the safe side) on a memory stick so that if your laptop fails you can use a colleague's
- Remind yourself that you have been asked to take on your present role. Believe in yourself more. Other colleagues have believed in you enough, so have some confidence in yourself!
- Be confident in your own style. Your way of dealing with your job is just that: your own, and it is as valid as anyone else's. You don't have to follow the style of your predecessor exactly

Deal with nerves

Almost everyone is nervous in some aspects of their job. For example, I admit that I am nervous before nearly every presentation I give and every time I have to speak in public. I have found the following helpful:

- If you're giving a presentation, practise what you will say in advance (especially the beginning and end). Practising beforehand helps you realize you need to work hard at choosing the right words and also lets you know how long the presentation will last
- Focus on other people, not yourself. If you are giving a presentation, as soon as the participants begin to arrive, start talking to them. As you do this, often your own nervousness will decrease
- Accept your nervousness
- Watch out for warning signs that affect you personally: e.g. stomach rumbling (or worse), dry throat, shallow breathing, tension in your body, fast heartbeat

- Learn what works for you to reduce tension: e.g. sipping water, taking deep breaths, eating and drinking sensibly, having a plan
- Practise the relaxation techniques that work for you, e.g. walking, deep breathing
- Have adequate sleep
- Wear comfortable clothing that you feel at ease in
- Have a support group of close friends who you can text: they can offer help and support
- Visualize how you will feel at the end of a difficulty
- Reward yourself with a treat: I find the thought of eating a bar of chocolate at the end of the presentation sometimes helps me through the day

(For further ways of dealing with stress, see Chapter Seven: Saturday.)

Motivate yourself

Ways in which you can motivate yourself include the following:

- Accept yourself and the difficult situation you are in: you cannot do anything to change the past or present, but you can do something about *your response to* your present situation
- Look back at past successes, however small: remind yourself of past achievements and think about how you achieved them
- Learn from others; take advice – have a coach / mentor (look back at Chapter Two: Monday)
- Do something, however small, even if you don't feel like it. Don't just sit there feeling sorry for yourself. Focus on the next thing you need to do in order to achieve your goal in order to make your goal a reality. Remember the saying: the journey of a thousand miles begins with one step. It might be researching an online course of study or emailing someone or calling someone by phone. Do something!
- Focus on results, not activity. Set yourself a target to see how much you can achieve in ten minutes, then repeat that ten minutes later

- Have close friends who can support and encourage you
- Try to remain positive. Even in the face of difficulty, there is always hope
- Don't allow yourself to become irritated by minor things: think of far greater injustices in the world
- Don't take someone's comments about your work personally. Become more resilient. The intention behind their remarks is for you to work better. Look to see how you can rise above your emotions, humbly accept your errors, take responsibility and do your best to improve
- Think what your family, e.g. your parents, went through to help you reach where you are today

 Don't wait until you feel motivated – sometimes you just have to push yourself.

See also dealing with procrastination in Chapter Three (Tuesday).

Not giving up hope

Tara had had a difficult life. Her dad had just died and she looked after her mother, brother and sister. She didn't give up hope, however. She asked friends to help her and she studied hard. Eventually she was able to get a job abroad and send money back to her family. By not feeling sorry for herself and by constantly taking the initiative, she did not give up hope but remained positive. Through hard work, she became successful.

Summary

Today we've seen that we cannot ignore emotions. You may need to explore your own emotional make-up and consider how emotional you are.

Positively, we have seen that you need to:

- Realize you cannot change what has happened, but you can change your response to it
- Take responsibility for your own actions
- Move beyond blaming others: reframe
- Have courage
- Become more resilient
- Work on your own character to overcome difficulties
- Be positive: think what can you do and begin to do that
- Do something, however small. Every step is a step forward
- Don't be self-centred; consider others

Exercise

1 How would you describe your own emotional make-up?
2 Do you allow your thoughts to control your emotions or vice versa? Think of times when

SUNDAY MONDAY TUESDAY WEDNESDAY THURSDAY FRIDAY SATURDAY

you have allowed your emotions to control your thoughts. How would you act differently now with hindsight?

3 Think of one emotion – e.g. fear, jealousy or insecurity – that affects you strongly. What positive steps can you take to deal with it?

Fact-check

1. I have strong feelings, so I:
a) need to pretend they don't exist and ignore them ❑
b) spend all my time thinking only about them ❑
c) need to express them in a safe context ❑
d) need to express them constantly. ❑

2. Knowing your own emotional make-up is:
a) a waste of time ❑
b) 'Shut up!' ❑
c) the only thing that counts. ❑
d) useful ❑

3. The way to manage your feelings is to:
a) emphasize them ❑
b) drink more juice ❑
c) manage your thoughts ❑
d) ignore them. ❑

4. Discussing feelings:
a) is a waste of time ❑
b) can be important ❑
c) could become unpleasant so I avoid it ❑
d) is the most important thing in the world ❑

5. I challenge assumptions:
a) where appropriate ❑
b) never ❑
c) always, so that's all that I do ❑
d) what's an assumption? ❑

6. If someone is expressing their feelings, you should:
a) interrupt them ❑
b) tell them to stop and calm down ❑
c) avoid them ❑
d) let them do so. ❑

7. Reframing is:
a) seeing something positive from a negative perspective ❑
b) seeing something negative from a positive perspective ❑
c) what you do to old photographs ❑
d) introducing change management. ❑

8. When I am in a difficult situation:
a) I blame other people ❑
b) I don't do anything ❑
c) I take responsibility and choose how to respond ❑
d) I think only about my difficulty constantly. ❑

9. I'm not a confident person, so:
a) I buy more and more books on increasing my self-confidence ❑
b) I need to work at changing myself more ❑
c) I cannot do anything about it ❑
d) I will become increasingly insecure as I get older. ❑

10. When I don't feel motivated:
a) I think only about my past failures ❑
b) I eat more ❑
c) I pity myself for a whole week ❑
d) I make myself do something ❑

FRIDAY

Manage your relationships successfully

Introduction

SUNDAY / MONDAY / TUESDAY / WEDNESDAY / THURSDAY / FRIDAY / SATURDAY

> *'The simple act of paying positive attention to people has a great deal to do with productivity.'*
> Tom Peters (1942–), American writer on business management.

You are called upon to manage yourself, but a significant part of your working life will be with colleagues. How can you manage your relationships with them?

Today we will look at the importance of:

- Building good rapport and trust
- Listening more carefully
- Asserting yourself
- Managing conflict
- Managing your boss so you can work well with them
- Motivating your staff: a significant part of your work is to focus on others, to develop their skills
- Not neglecting family and friends

85

Build good rapport

For me, the key to establishing good rapport with people – a sense of mutual respect, trust and understanding – is to listen to them.

As a manager, you will need to do a lot of listening: to your boss as they direct your work, to colleagues as you talk about your work, in meetings as you discuss a range of subjects and make decisions, as you interview staff, solve problems and use the phone.

There are many reasons why listening is difficult:

- We tend to focus on what we want to say; by contrast, listening demands that our concentration is on someone else as we follow the sequence of their thoughts
- The person we're listening to may speak unclearly, too fast or repeat themselves
- The person we're listening to may be a non-native speaker and so does not speak in standard English
- We were probably not taught to listen. I vaguely remember school lessons trying to teach us reading, writing and speaking but I don't think I was ever taught to listen (or maybe I wasn't listening during those lessons!)

But listening is a really valuable skill. Have you ever felt really burdened by something and opened your heart to someone else? At the end you feel relieved and can say, 'Thank you for listening.'

The importance of listening

Listening:

- Focuses on the other person. Often when someone else is talking, we're focusing on thinking about what we are going to say as a reply
- Values the person you are listening to as an individual in their own right. This will help you understand why they are working or speaking as they are
- Helps you understand the point at which a person is. For example, if you are trying to sell something to customers,

you want to build a good relationship with them. By listening, you will discern who is interested and who is not, so you can use your time more valuably and concentrate on the more likely potential clients

- Encourages you to ask the right questions. As you focus on the other person, you will want to know more. We can distinguish:
  - Closed questions: ones that can be answered by a straight 'Yes' or 'No': 'Was the project late?' 'Yes.' 'Will you be able to give me the figures by 5 pm?' 'No.'
  - Open questions: ones that get people talking. Open questions begin with *why*, *how*, *who*, *when*, *where*, *what*. 'Why do you think the project is running late?' 'Because we didn't plan enough time for the extra work the customer now wants.'
- Means that you do not listen only to the words a colleague is speaking: you can perceive their response to what you are saying by being sensitive to their body language and tone of voice
- Allows you to 'listen between the lines', to become aware of any underlying messages that the speaker isn't able to verbalize
- Allows you to distinguish between facts and opinions. You will hear both, and you can discern what is objective information and what are the subjective thoughts on such information. You are then in a position to evaluate what has been said
- Enables you to gather information so that you can solve problems and make decisions more effectively
- Builds trust between people: you show that you are genuinely interested in them. This forms the basis to help you work well with them. Listening often improves relationships
- Offers an opportunity to develop more all-round relationships. For example. if a colleague says, 'I'm off on holiday tomorrow,' you can either ignore that signal (but ignoring it is possibly slightly rude), or you can use that as a hint that he or she wants to tell you more about themselves: 'Great, where are you going to?' 'Hong Kong'. You can then

remember to ask them, 'How was Hong Kong?' when you next see them

- Can resolve disagreements. If colleagues are in conflict with one another, listening to and understanding the opinions of either, or both, sides – whilst not necessarily agreeing with them – is an important first step in settling a disagreement
- Helps you understand people better. As you listen carefully to someone, you will discover more about that person: what is important to him or her, how they think and what they are feeling. Having such knowledge helps you work better with them, even if you don't like them or agree with their opinions

---

Susie was angry

Susie was angry. She worked late every evening to complete her tasks in the project but she felt her work was not appreciated or valued. It was only when a new colleague, Jan, started to work alongside her that something happened. Jan was concerned less about herself and her own work (which she did well) and more about her colleague – she cared enough to stop and listen to Susie. Susie was in tears as she poured out her heart to Jan, telling her about the real pressures she was working under. At the end of their conversation Susie told Jan, 'Thanks for listening. You're the first person I've been able to talk to about these things.' Having someone to talk to who truly listened to Susie really helped her, and she started to feel better.

Tips on better listening

Here are some ways to help you improve your listening skills:

- Be responsible. Realize that listening is an active skill and as such is hard work. Concentrate. For example, when I meet someone for the first time, I listen particularly attentively to catch their name. If I think I've heard it accurately, I'll say it back to them, e.g. 'Great to meet you, Nick!' If I didn't hear their name properly, I'll say, 'I'm sorry I didn't quite catch your name' or ask (if it is unusual to me and seems difficult to spell), 'Could you spell that for me please?'

● Focus on the other person, not yourself. Don't be tempted to interrupt the other person while he or she is talking. Stop and really listen to what the other person is saying. Make eye contact with them. Notice their body language. Be interested in them. Rephrase what they've said in your own way to help you clarify the meaning in your own mind. For example, 'So what you're really saying is that we should have put in place more effective monitoring controls.' Such a rephrasing process is called 'reflective listening'

● Be willing to accept the reasoning and opinions of others as valid. Be willing to acknowledge that you may make false assumptions and may have prejudices

● Be flexible in your response. If you are truly focused on the other person rather than on yourself, you will have a variety of responses available to you

● Discern the main points of what is being said. Speakers may or may not structure their argument well. Often, in informal talks or meetings it can be difficult to distinguish between, for example, facts, opinions, examples and ideas. It is important to try to work out the speaker's main point(s)

● Do your best to remain attentive, even if the other person is not; do not become distracted

● Write down in note form if you need to remember what a speaker is saying and you might otherwise forget it. Making notes can help you concentrate and avoid the sense that 'things go in one ear and out of the other'

● Don't be afraid of silence. Silence is part of a conversation. It can be:
  - A junction: which way will a conversation turn?
  - A time to catch up and digest what has been said
  - An opportunity for the other person to express their thoughts further
  - An opportunity to reflect on what has been said

Management styles

At his interview, Harry was asked about which management style he adopted. Wisely he responded that he had several, to suit different occasions, the people he is managing and the tasks they are doing, rather than having a 'one-size-fits-all' approach.

So at times he said his style is democratic, involving the whole team in the decision-making process. He uses this especially in change-management situations when he wants the team to feel and be committed to change. At other times, particularly when dealing with very urgent matters, he is directional and simply has to tell people what to do ('The customer has changed his mind and wants new figures by 3 pm today'). He added that that wasn't his preferred style, however, preferring to give responsibility to his team members, together with training, support and clear instructions and trusting them to get on with the tasks using their own good judgment.

Assert yourself

Respect is two-way in a relationship and so it is important that colleagues show respect towards you as well as you showing respect to them.
Assertive communication is different from:

● Being passive: letting other people treat you badly
● Being aggressive: forcefully insisting on your own rights and treating others badly

Being assertive means that you will:

● Respect others' rights as well as your own and be fair to yourself as well as other people
● Be proactive rather than reactive; prepare well and be flexible. Sometimes you will need to be firm; at other times you need to be more restrained
● Focus on people's behaviour, not criticizing them or ignoring their identity
● Set boundaries
● Communicate firmly and confidently. At times you will need to be courageous and stand up for what you believe is right

We can consider assertiveness in two areas: saying no to further commitments – see Chapter Seven (Saturday) – and managing conflict.

Manage conflict

At times you are bound to meet conflict. Trust breaks down. Personalities clash. Each department wants to avoid the most cutbacks or wants a bigger slice of the budget.

Deal with conflict quickly; tackle the issues. Don't be cautious and fearful about speaking directly and clearly about difficulties.

I've found the books *Difficult Conversations: How to Discuss What Matters Most* (by Douglas Stone, Sheila Heen and Bruce Patton; Michael Joseph, 1999) and *The Peacemaker: A Biblical Guide to Resolving Personal Conflict* (by Ken Sande; Baker Books, 1991) very useful. The following is based on what those authors helpfully suggest:

- Distinguish the incident – what's happening/happened – from feelings about the incident. Consider separately:
- The incident – someone said something; someone is to blame. Try to focus on the real issue. Remain calm. Listen closely. Ask open questions. Understand other people's interests as well as your own
- Feelings about the incident, e.g. anger, hurt
- The identity of the person. Sometimes a person's identity, including their own self-worth, will feel threatened. Calmly affirm your respect for them
- Intervene sooner rather than later, i.e. don't let the situation become out of control
- Listen until the other person feels heard and you discover the core issue
- Discern and respect your colleague's point of view and intentions, even though you may disagree with them
- Look at the issue in a positive way; it can be helpful to refer to the values of your company or organization
- Treat your colleague with respect
- Do what you can to resolve the issue and maintain the relationship if possible: prepare and evaluate possible creative solutions to agree on the way forward

Manage your boss

The way you handle your boss is crucial. You need to understand what kind of person they are (e.g. what is important to them and their strengths and weaknesses) and how they work. Then you can adapt your style of working to suit them. Some bosses want a clear written statement of the facts of the case before a meeting; others may want you to give them the facts at the meeting. Some prefer a one-page summary; others a long, detailed report. Some prefer to communicate by phone, others by email.

> **TIP** *How you handle your boss is crucial: you need to know what kind of person they are and how they work and then adapt your style to suit them.*

- Discuss priorities with your boss and make decisions with them. Discuss what they want you to do, especially if they continue to give you task after task. Agree on your goals and then, when they give you an additional task, discuss with them whether that achieves the agreed goal or not. If necessary, give them the responsibility of making the decision: 'Actually, I'm working on [this project] now: what do you want me to do?' Learn to say no where necessary
- If you can see a problem that is likely to happen, alert your boss sooner rather than later, so that he/she is aware of it and can act accordingly before the matter becomes serious
- Discuss expectations with your boss. Don't assume you know what they want and that they know what you want
- Fill in the gaps in a supportive way. One boss I had was a poor communicator but I knew what he was trying to say, so in meetings I was able to express it more clearly than he could. In a meeting, if your boss cannot remember the details, then supply them. At the end of a meeting, summarize what you have to do. If your boss is not decisive and you know what the right decision is, help them along: 'We should do this, because ...'

- Focus on what you can do to move things forward: 'We can deliver the order to China on time if Kate helps us. Shall I ask her?' [rather than: 'We'll miss the deadline to deliver the order to China unless you ask Kate to help us']
- Don't come to your boss only with a problem; come with the problem and one or two possible solutions. You are closer to the issues; it is a better use of your time and your boss's if you do so: 'This is the problem ... and I think we could do either ... or ...'
- Prove that you are trustworthy in small things and your boss will delegate more to you. If you make a promise to complete something by a certain time, make sure you keep that promise

Dealing with an incompetent boss

Some bosses see themselves as important and perfect and they don't like to think their authority is being undermined. But the reality is that some bosses do not have the knowledge or skills to fulfil their jobs well. In fact, none of us is perfect and no-one knows all the answers. So realize that your boss has strengths and weaknesses. Here are some suggested tactics:

- Point out errors indirectly and tactfully. At times it may be appropriate to say, 'You may not have realized, but ...' or 'I'm sure it was an inadvertent error'
- Check your facts are accurate before criticizing your boss
- Discuss the difficulty and possible ways forward with a trusted colleague or friend who will keep the matter confidential
- Try all you can to avoid being disloyal to your boss when you are with colleagues
- As a last resort, go to your boss's boss

Motivate your staff

It's Thursday afternoon and members of your team have, it seems, stopped working and are discussing tonight's football match. You try to get them back to work, but fail. And it's like that all too often. How can you motivate your staff?

Someone who is well motivated is positive, does their job well and enthusiastically and wants more responsibility. Such a person can boost the morale of colleagues and help them work well. On the other hand, someone who is poorly motivated will not seem to care about their work. They may turn up late for work and complain about small details. Such a person can have a negative effect on other colleagues.

Here are some tips to motivate staff:

- Show your trust in your team members by giving them greater responsibility and delegating more of your own work to them (see Chapter Three: Tuesday)
- Allow them to become experts in an area. Early in my career of dictionary writing, my boss saw my interest and skill at checking long verb entries in a dictionary (e.g. *do, go, get, make, set*), gave me the responsibility of editing these and so I became an expert in explaining English idioms (e.g. *do up*, 'renovate', *get out of*, 'evade a duty')
- Delegate whole tasks where possible. I once delegated three different aspects of the same task to three different people, who all felt frustrated and unfulfilled at the thirds they were given
- Delegate work clearly. Do colleagues know exactly what is expected of them? Vague and unclear instructions not only demotivate colleagues but also waste time
- Show that you value them. Listen to them. Be available for them to bring their concerns to you. Understand them. Try to find out 'what makes them tick'. Talk *to* them (not *at* them). Find out what interests them outside work
- Show that you value their work. Affirm them and recognize their achievements:
  - In public by praising them in front of their colleagues and/or
  - In private, affirming they are a valuable member of the team. Even saying, 'Thank you, you did that well' is an acknowledgement of gratitude

- Bring in food or buy each of them little treats, e.g. chocolate.
- Issue certificates for achievements: it's amazing how competitive colleagues can be for a certificate
- Don't criticize individuals in public or in front of colleagues
- Don't remain aloof. At one organization I worked at, I didn't mix socially with colleagues and therefore had difficulties later. I learnt from my mistake and altered my behaviour in later jobs
- Work generally at good communications. Communicate with colleagues, both formally in meetings and informally as you walk down the corridor for a coffee break. By 'communicating' I mean *speaking*, not emailing or texting! Spend time informally talking to people (and remember their names). Don't look down on people. I recall a comment on a teacher friend years ago: 'He even talks to the cleaners.' If you need something in a hurry, you will already hopefully have built up a store of goodwill
- In group meetings, focus on building a team, constantly affirming the team's commitment to reach the goal and recognize their progress on the way
- Encourage uncooperative colleagues to try a new system if they are reluctant to follow it. Or even ask them if they could suggest new ways of solving a problem
- Know their strengths and weaknesses. Try as far as possible to make sure they are 'round pegs in round holes' rather than 'square pegs in round holes'. This may be difficult as there will always be aspects of work (perhaps unexciting administrative tasks) that it seems no-one wants to do
- Focus on specific, measurable and achievable (SMART) actions, not on vague ideas: look back at Chapter One (Sunday)
- Try to remain positive, even when doing a structured task. That structured task is a significant part of a bigger picture
- Offer coaching and opportunities for development to all colleagues in areas they need further help in
- If you have come to the end of a project, celebrate that fact by all going out for a meal
- Involve colleagues in decision making and setting budgets. If your company or organization is undergoing a period of

change, then involve your colleagues at an earlier, rather than a later, stage, explaining the issues to them. They will then feel valued

- Encourage them to make positive suggestions as to how to work more effectively
- Ask a trusted colleague to come with you to a meeting of other managers. Let them accompany you for a few meetings and then gradually delegate some of the responsibilities to them
- Be aware of colleagues who moan constantly, who find minor fault in everything. Keep focused on what you want to achieve and avoid becoming distracted and dragged down by the moaners
- Do all you can to ensure their work is interesting and challenging. No-one likes boring repetitive tasks. Make sure your colleagues' work contains at least some interesting tasks that will stretch them

---

Earning respect

Colin was promoted. He stood out among all the other colleagues as the most competent member of the team, so it was natural that he was chosen to be the team leader.

However, when Colin was promoted to that role, things did not go well. In his inexperience in leading, he thought that if he just told his team members to do something then they would do it immediately. He also tried to introduce too many changes too quickly. Talking it through with his mentor, he was told that first he had to earn respect from the individuals under him. He learnt the hard way that he had to demonstrate his leadership skills and introduce changes more gradually (his mentor had said, 'Go for "Evolution" not "Revolution"'), and then the team would be ready to commit themselves to his vision.

Don't neglect other relationships in your life

It is important not to neglect other relationships in your life such as family and friends. If you have children, make time for them. The story is told of a successful top executive who felt he had 'wasted' a day fishing with his son. The son, however, saw that as one of the best days of his life: his dad had spent a whole day with him. For more on other relationships outside work, see Chapter Seven (Saturday).

> *'No-one was ever heard to say on their death-bed, "I wish I had spent more time at the office".'*
>
> Rob Parsons, The Sixty Minute Father

Summary

Today we have considered practical ways of managing the relationships in your life. Keys include:

- Respecting and valuing people
- Listening to colleagues better
- Building trust
- Managing conflict professionally
- Asserting yourself: knowing when to be firm and when to be more restrained
- Communicating well
- Knowing your boss's emphases, strengths and weaknesses, and style of working, and adapting your style and work accordingly
- Making time for family and friends

Exercise

1 How good a listener do friends and colleagues say you are? Choose one aspect of better listening, e.g. making better eye contact or stopping interrupting someone, and practice it until it becomes automatic.

2 Think about your boss. What are their emphases, strengths and weaknesses? Their style of working? How can you better adapt your style to work more productively with them?

3 Think about an area of conflict at work. What can you do more to listen to people's different viewpoints and distinguish the incident from feelings about the incident? What questions of identity are at stake? What are the next steps for you to undertake?

SUNDAY

MONDAY

TUESDAY

WEDNESDAY

THURSDAY

FRIDAY

SATURDAY

Fact-check

1. Relationships at work are:
   a) very annoying ❏
   b) non-existent: I just shout at my colleagues all the time ❏
   c) all very easy ❏
   d) difficult at times, so I need to work at them ❏

2. As an aspect of communicating, listening is:
   a) essential ❏
   b) nice to have, if you have the time ❏
   c) a waste of time ❏
   d) a luxury ❏

3. Listening:
   a) makes colleagues proud ❏
   b) destroys people ❏
   c) builds trust ❏
   d) increases self-confidence ❏

4. Listening helps you:
   a) focus on yourself ❏
   b) understand people better ❏
   c) gossip more easily ❏
   d) disagree more knowledgeably ❏

5. Asserting yourself means:
   a) being forceful and aggressive ❏
   b) being firm and fair to yourself and others ❏
   c) letting others treat you badly ❏
   d) becoming more confident towards others ❏

6. The way to handle conflict is:
   a) shout more loudly ❏
   b) solve the problem as quickly as possible ❏
   c) listen so that you understand the issues ❏
   d) what? we don't have any conflict here ❏

7. The key to managing your boss well is to:
   a) know what is important to them, their strengths and weaknesses and their style of working ❏
   b) work without paying any attention to them ❏
   c) criticize them disloyally in front of others ❏
   d) praise them constantly ❏

8. A key to motivating staff is:
   a) never delegate any work to them ❏
   b) shout more loudly at them ❏
   c) let them go home early ❏
   d) give them greater responsibility. ❏

9. A further key to motivating staff is:
   a) recognize their achievements ❏
   b) constantly point out their mistakes ❏
   c) give work only to colleagues you like ❏
   d) never involve them in decision making. ❏

10. As regards my family:
    a) I think about them all the time when I am supposed to be concentrating on my work ❏
    b) they see me at weekends and on holiday: isn't that enough? ❏
    c) I don't know who they are ❏
    d) I make time for them ❏

SUNDAY

MONDAY

TUESDAY

WEDNESDAY

THURSDAY

FRIDAY

SATURDAY

SATURDAY

Manage stress thoroughly

Introduction

Stress can affect not only our work but also our whole life. Stress occurs where our body is called upon to do more than it can usually cope with.

Just as stress reveals itself in different ways in different people, so each one of us also needs to develop our own personal strategies for dealing with stress.

At times we all feel a little overwhelmed: answering emails, managing people, teams, policies and procedures, projects ... How can you avoid getting stressed out by everything?

Today we will look at:

- What stress is
- How stress shows itself
- How to deal with stress practically, e.g. by being more assertive and saying no
- Ways of adjusting your lifestyle to cope with stress

Acknowledge stress will come

Acknowledge that stress will come. In fact, a little stress may be good for you – some people work best with the pressure of an immediate deadline. However, if stress becomes out of control it can become a problem. Be alert to signs of stress in yourself.

Recognize stress

Times when stress may come:

● Difficult relationships	● Giving a presentation
● Financial problems	● Examinations
● Health issues	● Unrealistic deadlines
● Moving home	● Feeling undervalued
● Bereavement	● Traumatic events
● Starting a new job	● The threat of redundancy

Signs of stress include:

● Physical symptoms:	● Loss of appetite
● Inability to sleep properly	● Repetitive nervous actions such
● Aches, pains, tightness of	as nail-biting
muscles, headaches	● Using alcohol, tobacco, caffeine,
● Upset stomach, nausea	etc.
● Difficulty swallowing	● Putting on weight

Other symptoms:

● Becoming annoyed easily	● Constant feelings of
● Feeling like screaming	disappointment
● Finding yourself in tears	● Constant worry and anxiety
● Feeling helpless as things get out	Constant frustration with
of control	colleagues and work
● Isolating yourself from others and	● Not thinking straight; distracted,
becoming absorbed with yourself,	confused
not wanting to discuss matters	● Putting off making decisions
with others	● Unable to concentrate
● Constant low energy levels	● Unable to relax
● Deep, cynical attitude to work	● Loss of perspective: little
● Feeling overwhelmed as if things	problems become large
are completely beyond your	● Micromanaging: exercising too
control	much control
● Feeling bad about yourself,	● Focusing on unimportant details
questioning your abilities	● Making mistakes

How to deal with stress

Recognize that for certain periods in your life you may need not to do certain things at all. For example, a few years ago I spent six weeks solidly writing a significant part of a dictionary and reduced all personal commitments to an absolute minimum. At the end of that six-week period, I began to take on other commitments again.

If it all gets too much, visit your doctor. In the meantime, here are some ways of dealing with stress.

Communicate with colleagues more personally

Communicate more face to face with people. Getting to know people more deeply means more all-round relationships; you can defuse stress by talking to people, not by emailing them. Before the age of email, colleagues would get up from their desks and talk to a colleague. Of course, I'm aware of the benefits of email, but sometimes old-fashioned methods work well too. Speak to colleagues on the phone, too. Telephoning someone is a better way of building a relationship with someone than email or text messaging.

Sixteen practical ways of dealing with stress

1 Build in regular patterns of exercise and breaks
2 If you are looking at a computer screen for a long time, take a short break (e.g. five to ten minutes) every hour
 ● Physical exercise helps, however brief. Try to get some fresh air during the working day
 ● Join a gym; play sport. During the first few years of my working life I pushed myself too hard and became ill. I had to learn to take regular exercise. So I made myself take regular walks around the block of houses where I live: I have been walking round the block normally twice a day for 25 years. I have variations: I find the occasional walk in a nearby park at lunch particularly helpful

- Build in regular times off. Don't overfill every moment of your 24 hours. For example, if you're busy for two weeks, make sure in week three you have some personal slack time. Look forward to regular time off. One colleague deliberately sets himself something special to look forward to every six weeks

3 Talk problems over with friends. Plan in times to meet with people you like, rather than these who will drain you and reduce your energy reserves. You can share good things in your life as well as difficulties. As the proverb says: 'A trouble shared is a trouble halved': it often helps to discuss your problems with someone else. As someone who has been self-employed for most of my working life, I have had to deliberately make regular times (for me, mostly over lunch) for appointments with friends and colleagues to discuss life and work issues. At times, I have made myself open up and express myself on personal issues with friends to seek their advice, awkward though such experiences are. Some accountability is good for us

4 Take yourself less seriously. Another proverb states that 'Laughter is the best medicine'. Laughing is an excellent remedy to restore good health and keep well

5 Eat and drink sensibly. You know the rules – apply them! You can't remain healthy in the long term on a diet of junk food, and drinking and smoking excessively

6 Switch the TV/computer off earlier and get more sleep: if you can wake up without an alarm clock, then you are getting enough sleep

7 Have a life outside work. Bring some balance to your life. The proverb 'All work and no play makes Jack a dull boy' is a true one: people who do not make time for leisure activities risk damaging their health, the quality of their work and/ or their personal relationships. We all need to take a break from work. Spend time with your partner, family or friends. Join a club. Volunteer to help others

- Take up a hobby that is not related to your work. Volunteer to help others. Do something regularly that is not related to your work. A friend works in industry in a high-level job, but is always back home to spend Friday evenings at his model-railway club. Having an interest outside work helps you unwind and relax

- Take holidays without feeling guilty ... and without all your electronic gadgets! Take up other activities and be reminded what it is like to be human. These will give you fresh motivation, creativity and renewed energy. I know you will come back to hundreds of emails: a colleague sets her return to work on a Thursday for that reason, so that she can clear her emails ready for the following Monday, however the time off will do you more good than a clear inbox.

8 Don't overcommit yourself by making promises you know you cannot keep. Be realistic

9 Cut out aspects of your job that you do not need to do. I once met a colleague who was working on four projects that were far beyond the scope of his work, so I told him to stop work on all of them. He was so far immersed in one of them that he had to complete it, but he realized he could drop the other three

10 Discuss matters with your boss. Can you be relieved of some areas of work? Can some activities be delayed?

11 Focus on what you can do, and do that – a little is better than nothing

12 Talk things over with a coach or mentor. They can help you develop your career and work through the relevant issues (see Chapter Two: Monday)

13 Learn relaxation techniques for your body: many people find yoga helpful. Simple deep-breathing techniques can work wonders – focus on the positive in your mind.

14 Listen to music – whichever style helps you unwind and energizes you

15 Evoke the senses. When I am stressed, I try to think of one of two situations: the gentle lapping of water on a shore of a lake in Austria; sipping a cold cola in a restaurant in France. Both of these situations are memorable to me because they evoke the senses. What memories could you use?

16 Try not to let your work life affect your personal life. Do your best to leave work behind when you finish work. It is important to cultivate friendships with people outside work

Try to spend some time every day doing something you enjoy.

 Don't overcommit yourself by making promises you know you cannot keep. Be realistic.

Under pressure

Elaine was under pressure. She was actually doing two jobs, each taking up three days a week. She was getting very stressed and knew she could not continue doing such work indefinitely. She told her manager Ron at both informal one-to-ones and at the formal half-yearly appraisal she expressed the frustration she felt in her work. Unfortunately, Ron said he would act to resolve the difficulty, but over a period of several months nothing happened. He awkwardly avoided eye contact with her whenever they passed in the corridor.

Things turned out better, however, when Ron moved on and he was replaced by Sheila. Her motto was 'under promise and over deliver' so, for example, when she said she would check the financial data for the previous month by the end of week three in the following month, invariably she had completed it by the end of week two. Within a few weeks of Sheila taking on Ron's role, she had sorted out Elaine's work patterns to everyone's satisfaction. Soon Elaine began to enjoy her work again.

Learn to say no

Do you find it difficult to say no? Perhaps it's because you want to avoid confrontation, or because you want to be liked and appreciated, or you enjoy the feeling of being needed. However, no-one can do everything, so you will be doing yourself (and your work) a favour if you only take on work you can cope with. Here are some tips to help you say no:

● Be aware that others may be trying to make you feel guilty if you were to say no

- Say no sooner rather than later. Generally speaking, the more you delay something, the more difficult it could become to say no. Be more assertive
- Work at good relationships (see also Chapter Six: Friday) generally so that you know people well enough that they will not feel offended if you say no
- Be clear about your own role and priorities. Have these constantly in mind. Is what you are being asked to do a significant distraction from that? If so, then say no
- Be aware of what you have been trained to do. You may need to refuse to participate in a task or project that you have not been trained for. Other people in the team may be more able to do certain projects
- Be aware of your own values. If you are being asked to go beyond these (e.g. if you are asked to lie for your boss), then say no clearly
- Consider the effects of taking on further tasks. Would undertaking them lead to delays in fulfilling your existing commitments?
- Be reasonable towards yourself: you have a right to say no
- Practise making such responses as: 'I'd love to help, but I'm already fully committed/stretched.' You could add: 'I hope you find someone else who can help you.' 'I'm fairly busy but if you want to send me a short email letting me know exactly what you want and how you feel I could help, I'll look at it.'
- Suggest an alternative: 'I'm not really sure I'm the right person to deal with this. Why don't you ask ...?'
- If your boss is asking you to take on further responsibilities, put the onus back on him or her by asking which activity he or she wants you to tackle
- Discuss what precisely needs to be done
- Compromise on what needs to be done; negotiate: 'I'll cover your shift if you do mine on Saturday', but make sure they do so
- Don't apologize; don't say, 'I'll come back to you later if I find I have time,' because that adds to your already committed to-do list. Ask your colleague to come back to you later (fortunately, they probably won't). Or you could say, 'You could see if I'm less busy next week'

Saying no to further commitments

Bob felt flattered to be asked to join a committee to look at succession planning, but he wasn't sure. He felt he was already fully stretched and that a further commitment might just be too much. Over lunch with Mike, the chairman, they discussed the responsibilities of the role, which confirmed Bob's concerns, so he said no at that time. However, he added that he thought it likely his other commitments would lessen six months later when he was due to have an assistant who could cover some of his responsibilities. Sure enough, six months later, Mike asked Bob again and then, with some fresh capacity because he then had his assistant, Bob accepted the offer.

Summary

Today we have looked at stress and seen that it will affect us. We have considered how it might show itself and different ways of dealing with it. Key ways include:

- communicating with colleagues
- learning to say no
- living a healthy lifestyle
- having a life outside of work

Exercise

1 How does stress show itself in your life?
2 Think of a time when you have been stressed. How well did you cope with it?
3 How, on reflection, could you have coped with it better?
4 What can you do practically to reduce the stress you know you will face in the future?
5 Consider now, in advance, strategies for saying no to requests that you know will come in your work.
6 What three things have you learnt from reading this book?

SUNDAY MONDAY TUESDAY WEDNESDAY THURSDAY FRIDAY SATURDAY

Fact-check

1. Stress affects:
   a) no-one: what is the problem? ❑
   b) everyone: that is why we need to consider it ❑
   c) a few weak people ❑
   d) people who have now left the company ❑

2. Everyone suffers stress:
   a) happily ❑
   b) in different ways ❑
   c) in the same way ❑
   d) 24 hours a day, 365 days a year ❑

3. One way of dealing with stress is:
   a) to shout more loudly all the time ❑
   b) quit my job ❑
   c) become even more introverted ❑
   d) use email less and speak to people more ❑

4. Regular exercise:
   a) is a waste of time ❑
   b) helps reduce stress ❑
   c) is all I think about all the time ❑
   d) makes me even angrier ❑

5. Talking over difficulties with friends is:
   a) impossible, as I haven't got any friends I can talk to ❑
   b) a silly idea ❑
   c) very helpful ❑
   d) all I do ❑

6. Having finished this book, I will spend more time:
   a) compiling more to-do lists but never using them ❑
   b) planning my time more effectively ❑
   c) reading more books on being a manager ❑
   d) eating in the canteen ❑

7. Thinking time is:
   a) useful to help you become even more effective as a manager ❑
   b) wasted ❑
   c) all I do ❑
   d) nice if you have the time ❑

8. An important way to build better relationships is to:
   a) talk more ❑
   b) be silent more ❑
   c) listen more ❑
   d) eat more ❑

9. I realize I need to work harder at:
   a) only work relationships ❑
   b) only personal relationships ❑
   c) my own life ❑
   d) all relationships in life, both at work and outside work ❑

10. Since reading this book, I feel:
    a) even more arrogant because I never really needed it ❑
    b) more equipped to manage myself better ❑
    c) overwhelmed by even more to do ❑
    d) nothing at all ❑

Fact-check

SUNDAY
MONDAY
TUESDAY
WEDNESDAY
THURSDAY
FRIDAY
SATURDAY

113

Review what you have learnt this week

Look back at **Sunday**: do you know yourself? What aims do you have in life?

Look back at **Monday**: during the time when you can concentrate best, do you make sure that you focus on your key tasks?

Look back at **Tuesday**: can you plan your work and your diary even more effectively?

Look back at **Wednesday**: how can you manage your thoughts even better to make good decisions?

Look back at **Thursday**: are you becoming more resilient emotionally?

Look back at **Friday**: what relationships do you need to work harder at? How can you work more effectively with your boss?

Look back at **Saturday**: what can you do to alleviate stress? Can things be done differently?

7×7

1 Seven key ideas

- Know when – what time of day and which day of the week – you work best. Protect that time as far as possible for your key work that requires most concentration; don't say to yourself that you will just get a few smaller things out of the way first.

- Listen better to build trust in relationships.

- When planning, remember that the time spent doing admin is likely to be far more than you think.

- Don't wait until you feel motivated or you will wait forever. Push yourself.

- How you handle your boss is crucial. You need to know what kind of person they are and how they work, and then adapt your style to suit them.

- Don't overcommit yourself or make promises you know you cannot keep. Be realistic in your expectations of yourself … and others.

- Stay fresh: don't stagnate; keep changing and making progress. Continue to dream dreams.

2 Seven best resources

- Stephen Covey, *Seven Habits of Highly Effective People* (Simon & Schuster, 2004). First published in 1989, this is a highly influential management book.

- http://www.businessballs.com/ – Website offering fresh ideas on business training and organizational development.

- http://www.mindtools.com/ – Website helping users learn practical skills to become an effective manager and leader, e.g. on problem solving, decision making, time management and communication skills.

- http://www.businessknowhow.com/ – Website providing guidance on business ideas, marketing, leadership, etc.

- Brian Harris, *The Tortoise Usually Wins: Biblical Reflections on Quiet Leadership for Reluctant Leaders* (Paternoster, 2013). Written from a Christian perspective, exploring quiet leadership from the viewpoint of those who by temperament are quiet, reluctant leaders.

- http://www.peterfuda.com/ – Website of Dr. Peter Fuda, a leading authority on business and leadership transformation.

- http://www.ted.com/ – TED talks: a non-profit organization with the aim of spreading ideas, especially in the form of short, powerful talks (18 minutes or less).

3 Seven things to avoid

- Poor time management: not delegating enough; having unrealistic expectations of yourself and others.

- Micromanaging: managing a task or people (including yourself) in a way that is too detailed. Concentrate on the big picture.

- Not being focused: doing too many things badly.

- Poor relationships: focusing on wanting people to like you rather than being an effective team leader.

- Being overcome by stress too often.

- Thinking that your job is to keep things running smoothly rather than initiating change.

- Not regularly reviewing what you do against clear priorities and objectives.

4 Seven inspiring people

- Tony Buzan, inventor of mind maps who has developed techniques to help people think more creatively. See http://www.thinkbuzan.com.

- Stephen Covey, for his influential book *Seven Habits of Highly Effective People.*

- Daniel Goleman, for his significant books *Emotional Intelligence* (Bantam Books, 1995; Bloomsbury, 1996) and *Focus: the hidden driver of excellence* (Harper Collins USA, 2013; Bloomsbury, 2013)

- John Kotter, for his work on leading change management, e.g. *Leading Change* (Harvard Business School, 1996). See also http://www.kotterinternational.com.

- Edward de Bono, for his work on creative and lateral thinking, e.g. *Six Thinking Hats* (Little Brown and Company, 1985). See also http://www.debonogroup.com.

- John Maxwell, writer and speaker on leadership. See http://www.johnmaxwell.com.

- Mike Bechtle, expert on practical communication. See http://www.mikebechtle.com.

5 Seven great quotes

- 'The best preparation for good work tomorrow is to do good work today.' Elbert (Green) Hubbard (1856–1915), American businessman, writer, and printer.

- 'Remember that time is money.' Benjamin Franklin (1706–90), American statesman, scientist, and author.

- 'Any committee is only as good as the most knowledgeable, determined and vigorous person on it. There must be somebody who provides the flame.' Claudia (Lady Bird) Johnson (1912–2007), widow of former US President, Lyndon B Johnson.

- 'In an information-rich world, the wealth of information means a dearth of something else: a scarcity of whatever it is that information consumes. What information consumes is rather obvious: it consumes the attention of its recipients. Hence a wealth of information creates a poverty of attention and a need to allocate that attention efficiently among the overabundance of information sources that might consume it.' Herbert A. Simon (1916–2001), American psychologist and economist.

- 'The simple act of paying positive attention to people has a great deal to do with productivity.' Tom Peters (1942–), American writer on business management.

- 'Success is that old ABC – ability, breaks and courage.' Charles Luckman (1909–99), American architect.

- 'No-one was ever heard to say on their death-bed, "I wish I had spent more time at the office"' Rob Parsons, founder Care for the Family, *The Sixty Minute Father.*

6 Seven things to do today

- Check your progress through the day by looking at your to-do list.

- At the end of today, write tomorrow's to-do list; at the end of your working week, plan the major tasks you want to achieve each day of the following week.

- Put in your diary time to think, or better still put in your diary three times to think. Two may drop out, but make sure you keep one of them.

- Put in your diary every month a review to check your progress in your short-, medium- and long-term goals.

- Put in your diary time with family and friends and breaks (holidays).

- Begin to tackle a major task you have been putting off. The first task may be to list some of the things you need to do. If so, begin to do that, putting realistic dates by each step. In other words, do something, however small. Every step is a step forward.

- Try to plan in some time every day doing something you enjoy.

7 Seven trends for tomorrow

- Administration will constantly try to take over your life. Do what you need to do, but make sure you do at least the minimum.

- Technology will constantly produce innovations. Make sure technology saves you time.

- Thinking time will get squeezed out: *make* time to think.

- Increasingly large organizations will develop as companies merge and buy one another out: know your role; play to your strengths as far as you can.

- Unimportant things will try to take over your life: make sure you set priorities and manage well the time you can control.

- The number of meetings will go on increasing: know the purpose of every meeting you go to; make sure the actions are well written up so that you and your colleagues know clearly what actions to take and by when.

- More and more communications will be undertaken by email. Remember the more personal ways of communicating in person or by phone.

Answers to fact-check questions

Chapter 1
b c a d d c b c d a

Chapter 2
a d c b a d b c c b

Chapter 3
b d b c c c a d a b

Chapter 4
c b a d a b b d b c

Chapter 5
c d c b a d b c b d

Chapter 6
d a c b b c a d a d

Chapter 7
b b d b c b a c d b